Cooking the Dutch Oven Way

"Cooking the Dutch Oven Way *will erase any hesitation you've ever had about cooking crowd-pleasing food over a campfire. . . . From wild game to a fresh catch, Woodruff has a simple preparation for today's active outdoor family.*"

—Elizabeth Norfleet, Editor, *Taste-Full Magazine*

Cooking the Dutch Oven Way

Third Edition

By

Woody Woodruff

Revised by

Ellen Woodruff Anderson and

Jane Woodruff

The Globe Pequot Press

GUILFORD, CONNECTICUT

Cover photos: © 1999 Glenn Oakley
Cover design: Adam Schwartzman
Text design: Nancy Freeborn

Library of Congress Cataloging-in-Publication Data
Woodruff, Woody.
    Cooking the dutch oven way / by Woody Woodruff.— 3rd ed. / rev. by
Ellen Anderson and Jane Woodruff.
        p. cm.
    ISBN 0-7627-0669-4
    1. Dutch oven cookery. I. Anderson, Ellen. II. Woodruff, Jane. III. Title.

TX840.D88 W66 2000
641.5'89—dc21

                                                00-025084

Manufactured in the United States of America
Third Edition/Seventh Printing

To Mom and Dad

Grace:

For Food
For Raiment
For Life
For Opportunity
For Friendship and Fellowship
We Thank Thee, Oh Lord

Contents

Foreword

Wouldn't it be incredible to know someone who had reinvented the wheel? Well, the late Woody Woodruff didn't invent a new design for a wheel, but he did invent a better Dutch oven.

Woody was a Dutch oven master. He fine-tuned his cooking technique during a half century of training Boy Scout leaders, demonstrating open-fire and charcoal cooking hundreds of times. His innovation—perfecting a new rectangular design for the traditionally round Dutch oven—earned him international fame. Woody demonstrated his mastery of outdoor cooking at scouting programs in Trinidad, Jamaica, Guyana, and Canada as well as the United States. Further, he was certified as a Scoutmaster training expert by scouting's international headquarters at Gilwell Park, England.

Woody's greatest accomplishment in his outdoor education career was his development of remarkable recipes for outdoor cooking. While these recipes are ideal for Dutch oven cooking, they are useful for any situation where a one-pot dish is appropriate. Frankly, I hate cleaning up utensils and having to work with large fires, so one-pot cooking is always appropriate for me. Trading the hassles of multiple cooking pots for the ease of finding a recipe that you can throw together into just one vessel—and of having a meal that basically cooks itself—makes this book a boon for any busy (or lazy) cook.

Woody's one-pot meals go beyond main-course dinner concoctions. Breakfast meals, desserts, breads, cakes—they are all here. Specific menus include fish, poultry, vegetables . . . and meats. And oh, what meats! All types and combinations. Just to read these recipes is enough to get your salivary glands working.

Woody suffered a heart attack late in life that caused him to make a major revision in his recipes. He created the first "heart smart" Dutch oven meals with low-fat, low-cholesterol ingredients, which were included in the book's second edition. This tradition has continued with this third edition of newly revised and annotated recipes.

Since its first publication twenty-four years ago, Woody's *Cooking the Dutch Oven Way* has been a best seller in outdoor literature. It fulfills a significant niche in outdoor lore as well as specialized cooking literature. And it provides all outdoor travelers with both traditional and modern recipes and techniques to fully enjoy one of the most enjoyable methods of cooking outdoors—cooking the Dutch oven way!

William W. Forgey, M.D.
Friend and Dutch oven co-cooker

Among other duties, Dr. Forgey is currently the president of the Wilderness Medical Society and a member of the Boy Scouts of America National Health and Safety Committee as well as the Northern Tier High Adventure Program.

Introduction

The recipes that I have brought together in the following pages are reflections of the time since 1920 when I went on my first overnight with a number of friends. My father and the other adult slept on a bedspring and mattress they had brought along in the Model T truck and placed on the ground. The rest of us slept on the ground with an assortment of blankets and covers made into bedrolls. Sleeping bags were scarce in those days.

Our cooking was quite elaborate. Dad buried potatoes in the coals and smoked up a number of Mother's pots and pans in the ordeal of preparing the meal for fifteen or twenty hungry boys. We ate well, but what a mess to clean up, and what a lot of time wasted!

Since that time it has been in the back of my mind to keep cooking on the camping trail as simple as possible, with the least amount of cleanup.

I've demonstrated Dutch oven cooking from Hawaii to the East Coast and from Canada to South America—many times. And I found that we all have the same problem—we like to eat and eat well. Really, now—no one likes to eat burned or poorly prepared food and then spend hours cleaning up the mess made from the catastrophes.

Naturally, we laugh about the bad experiences, but they have probably discouraged more new campers from going out a second time than any one other thing, including bugs. I have therefore dedicated myself to reviving the art of Dutch oven cooking, which is nearly dead in many parts of our country but is now making a comeback.

The pioneers must have eaten well. Most of them carried along cast-iron round ovens on their wagons, and most later kept these ovens near their fireplaces and used them regularly. The Dutch oven was a prized possession. This is probably the easiest method of preparing food that has ever been devised, even though it started four thousand or more years ago with earthenware and reed Dutch ovens.

For years I have had the fun of sharing Dutch oven cooking with hundreds of younger, middle-aged, and older people. Through the

1

experiences I have had in helping them, I have learned much about this culinary art. I'd like to offer you the following information to help you enjoy one of the finest ways of getting the best taste and most nourishment out of good food, with the easiest and simplest techniques— Dutch oven cooking.

I've tried to present this information in a way that will start a beginner in the easiest way possible; the rest is up to you. As your skill in oven use develops, you can rely on the many recipes for one-pot meals that you will find scattered throughout many cookbooks. I have tried and tested all of the recipes in this book, so I know they are simple enough for the beginner.

I have made no attempt to cover the complete field of all recipes. Instead I have selected a few basic types with various common ingredients. I hope to satisfy a need in the present day, when so many of us wish to be outdoors—either in the backyard or in our trailer down the road or camping on the trail.

With this start you will be well on your way to using the Dutch oven for any recipe available to you.

I have made no attempt to standardize the yields of these recipes, but I do find that most will serve 6 to 8 people. All the recipes can be easily adjusted for the size of the group by adjusting all ingredients proportionately.

If you find you are not interested in using a Dutch oven as such, all of these recipes can be used equally well in a casserole or baking dish in the regular oven.

No attempt has been made to compete with any other author on recipes or methods. I have developed them through all my associations with many, many friends interested in good cooking, and I want to pass them on to you.

Woody Woodruff, 1988

> **Throughout this book you'll find recipes marked with the "heart smart" icon. These low-fat, low-salt, low-cholesterol dishes can make cooking the Dutch oven way as healthful as it is easy.**
>
> **= Heart Smart**

Selecting, Using, and Caring for Your Dutch Oven

In years past cast iron was the only reasonably priced Dutch oven material available. Today we also have aluminum, which does the job every bit as well, is only about a third as heavy, is less apt to break in handling due to its weight, and is easier to clean. Choose whichever material you feel you will be most comfortable with. All Dutch ovens, however, should have legs at least 1½ inches high and a lid with a lip that seals well. Extension legs are available for the rectangular and square ovens intended for use with wood or other noncharcoal heat sources. You can also extend the legs by placing them on ground, metal, or stones.

The lid or bottom of the Dutch oven also work well for open-fire frying or cooking. Use the same precautions you'd follow with other frying pans or cooking vessels.

To prepare a *cast-iron* Dutch oven for use, it should be thoroughly washed and cleaned in regular dishwater, then immediately rinsed and dried. Completely coat it inside and out with no-salt cooking oil and place in the kitchen oven at 250° to 300°; in 2 or 3 hours your Dutch oven will be ready to use. If the household oven is not available, use charcoal under and on top of your Dutch oven (just as is recommended for cooking) for 2 or 3 hours for the same results.

You can use cast-iron Dutch ovens for many years and for many different dishes. Wash them each time you use them in regular dishwater. Then warm them up and coat them with cooking oil while they are hot, or heat the oil and swab it on.

If rust appears on a cast-iron oven, it should be washed, heated up, and treated as soon as possible. You may have to use steel wool, a wire brush, or sandpaper to get the rust off.

Cast-aluminum Dutch ovens are also fine pieces of cookware and should be washed and dried after use, just as aluminum cooking utensils, but *they need no other preparation or treatment* before or after use.

3

Store either type of oven top-down with air space underneath and the lid right-side up on top of the legs.

Crucial to the operation of your Dutch oven is controlling the heat. Once you understand this process, you can effectively bake and cook even in a tin can.

Start charcoal at the edge of the campfire, then lift it with tongs or a shovel to the oven.

Starting charcoal without liquid fuels or electric starters is easy. Make a starter from a number 10 (16-ounce) or larger tin can by putting a row of 1-inch holes around its bottom for draft. Crumple up one double sheet of newspaper and lay it in the bottom of the can. Place a piece of expanded metal or chicken wire, cut to the size of the can's inside, on the paper, then pour the charcoal on top. Light the paper, and in a very few minutes the coals will be ready to transfer to the oven.

Fine patented charcoal lighters available. They really do a good job, are not expensive, and last a long time. One double sheet of crumpled newspaper under the hinged grate of the charcoal lighter will get the charcoal lit in 8 minutes. The charcoal can be dropped out of the bottom for grill cooking or can be transferred to the Dutch oven with tongs or shovel.

After the initial charcoal is put on and under the oven, you can add unlit coals as needed; they will start rapidly when they contact the lit ones.

When using wood to make charcoal, hardwoods such as oak, cherry, apple, or hickory will give you the best results. When using softwoods you have to stand over the oven almost constantly to feed the fire, and even then the fuel won't be as consistently hot or stable.

TOOL AND EQUIPMENT NEEDS

A few tools and pieces of equipment are essential for Dutch oven cooking:

- Charcoal starter
- 16- or 18-inch charcoal tongs
- Small, short-handled shovel
- Cooking pliers
- Oven-lid hook made from a green, forked stick (necessary for some ovens)
- Pair of heavy-duty oven mitts or pads
- Fire extinguisher—either a commercial model or a bucket of sand or water

It is best to build a small fire beside the oven and keep shoveling the freshly made charcoal from there to the oven.

If you're using the 4-inch extension legs available for the square and rectangular Dutch ovens, it's best to have a pile of small hardwood, pencil size or larger, cut ahead.

A word of caution: You can easily burn food in the oven by letting a twig fire grow too hot. Twigs ¼ to ½ inch in diameter can create enough heat to bake, boil, or fry in the oven, but the fire must be regularly fed.

If you're a beginner, start with charcoal briquettes to get the feel of the oven, using the temperature control chart on page 6 for *approximate* temperatures. Charcoal varies in heating quality; also, high winds will cause the fuel to burn faster.

When you're using two ovens, you can stack one on top of the other to take advantage of the heat. If you do this, remove some of the coals between the two ovens to regulate the heat.

In high wind or rain, you can shield the oven by setting it down on a piece of aluminum foil large enough to come up completely around and over the top of the Dutch oven, with enough left over for a double fold with the two ends together. Use the same amount of coals under and on top of the oven as suggested in the chart.

The temperatures listed on the chart are fairly accurate, but may fluctuate under various conditions. For instance, charcoal varies considerably, and charcoal made from hardwoods does a better job than the mineral product. The oven can be heated in a number of ways, including in the kitchen oven, in a fireplace with wood ash charcoal, with small twigs or buffalo chips, with whale or seal oil, or with canned heat.

Temperatures outside will affect the oven very little if you've protected it from wind and rain. Indeed, you should be able to use it in weather from -20° to 100° with no more than a 5-minute difference in baking times!

TEMPERATURE CHART
Charcoal Briquette Count

This chart was developed to give the beginner a fairly accurate picture of how many charcoal briquettes to start with. The temperatures achieved will vary due to charcoal quality, wind, and other weather elements.

	ALUMINUM				CAST IRON			
	6½ x 9"		9 x 9"		8" round		12" round	
OVEN TEMP	Under	Top	Under	Top	Under	Top	Under	Top
250°–300°	4	6	6	8	2	4	3	5
300°–350°	5	7	7	10	3	5	4	6
350°–400°	6	8	8	12	4	6	5	7
400°–450°	7	9	9	14	5	7	6	8

GENERAL INFORMATION FOR DUTCH OVEN RECIPE PLANNING

Measurements

3 teaspoons = 1 tablespoon

2 tablespoons = 1 fluid ounce

4 tablespoons = ¼ cup

16 tablespoons = 1 cup

1 cup = 8 fluid ounces

Butter or Margarine

¼ stick = 2 tablespoons

½ stick = ¼ cup

1 stick = ½ cup

4 sticks = 2 cups (1 pound)

Many ¼ pound stick wrappers are marked with these measurements

Beef and Pork

Beef

Four-Pound Boneless Beef Roast, 8
Granddad Woody's Corned Beef, 9
Tasty Beef Roast, 10
Salisbury Steak, 11
Heart Smart Meat Loaf, 12
Oven-Easy Meat Loaf, 13
Ground Beef Balls, 14
Mini Meal Sirloin Balls, 15
Round Steak and Potato Pie, 16
Beef Round, 17
Beef-Bean Oven Dish, 17
Beef Main Dish, 18
Beef-Macaroni Cheesit, 19
Beef-Noodle Oven Dish, 20
Beef-Tomato-Potato One Pot, 21
Chili, 21
Kidney Beans with Beef, 22
Meat and Potato Casserole, 23
Oven Hash, 24
Veal Stew with Noodles, 25
Pork-Beef Shish, 26

Pork

BBQ Pork Chops Dutch Oven Style, 27
Pork Chop Bake, 28
Pork Chops Old-Home Style, 29
Mushroomed Pork Steak, 30
Country-Style Spare Ribs, 31
Kraut and Spare Ribs Country Style,
31

Ham

Ham and Potato Bake, 32
Ham and Corn Bake, 32

Bacon

Bacon Bake, 33
Bacon-Bean Oven Dish, 33

Sausage and Hot Dogs

Meal in an Oven, 34
Sausage Roll, 34
Sausage-Cheese Balls, 35
Sausage-Cheese Biscuits, 35
Sausage-Rice Oven Dish, 36
Egg-Dog Bake, 37
Sauerkraut and Hot Dogs, 38

FOUR-POUND BONELESS BEEF ROAST

325°

Oven time: Preheat 10 minutes
Bake 2–2¼ hours

1. Remove the lid of the Dutch oven after preheating, and place the roast inside.

2. Sear the roast by making sure that all parts of it touch the bottom of the Dutch oven long enough to turn gray. This will help hold in the roast's juices.

3. Add salt and pepper to taste.

4. Place the lid on the oven and go away for a least a half hour.

5. Add six new pieces of charcoal on top of the oven and two under it. Let the roast cook for 45 minutes more.

6. Add two more pieces on top, and two beneath. Continue cooking to your choice of doneness.

BUYING MEATS

Look for meats that are bright in color, moist, and odor-free. The fat should be creamy white and firm. The highest-quality beef is marbled—thin lines of fat run through the meat.

GRANDDAD WOODY'S CORNED BEEF

350°

Oven time: 1½ hours per pound

3 gallons water
Salt
1 egg (for measuring)
½ pound brown sugar
3 garlic cloves
2 or 3 bay leaves (as you prefer)
1 box pickling spice, approximately 1¾ ounces
2 ounces saltpeter (can be bought at a drugstore)
15–20 pounds beef *

1. Add salt to the water until an egg floats.

2. Add the brown sugar, garlic, bay leaves, pickling spice, and saltpeter.

3. Cure beef in this brine in the refrigerator for 10 to 12 days, stirring every 3 or 4 days so that all sides receive same brine exposure.

4. To bake, place corned beef in a Dutch oven and cover with water. Use enough coals to simmer 1½ hours per pound, keeping water well over the meat at all times.

Almost any cut of beef will cure, but I prefer round steak, which has less waste and is delicious.

TASTY BEEF ROAST

350°

Oven time: 30–45 minutes per pound

1 3–5 pound beef roast
1 10¾-ounce can cream of mushroom soup
1 package dry onion soup mix

1. Preheat a Dutch oven.

2. Brown the roast.

3. Pour half the can of soup around the meat.

4. Pour the onion soup mix over the meat, then top with the remaining mushroom soup.

5. Bake to desired doneness.

Variation: Round steak may be used. Melt 1 stick (½ cup) margarine on top of the steak.

PLANNED-OVERS

When you cook meats, cook enough to be served more than once. A roast, for instance, can provide enough meat for sandwiches, hash, or pie.

 **SALISBURY STEAK**

350°

Oven time: 1 hour

8 ounces 90 percent lean ground beef or turkey
1 tablespoon dried onion flakes
1 teaspoon dried parsley flakes
14 small fat-free soda crackers, crumbled
¼ cup skim milk
1 12-ounce jar fat free beef gravy
2 teaspoons Worcestershire sauce
2 tablespoons light catsup
¼ teaspoon black pepper

1. Combine the meat, onion flakes, parsley flakes, cracker crumbs, and skim milk.

2. Form into four patties and place in a Dutch oven.

3. In a small bowl, combine the gravy, Worcestershire sauce, catsup, and black pepper.

4. Spoon this gravy mix over the meat patties and bake.

HEART SMART MEAT LOAF

350°

Oven time: 1 hour

1 pound 90 percent lean ground beef or turkey
1 cup quick oats
¾ cup chopped onion
1 teaspoon parsley flakes
1 teaspoon prepared mustard
1 tablespoon light brown sugar
1 10¾-ounce low-fat tomato soup

1. Combine all the ingredients.

2. Pat into a Dutch oven.

3. Bake 1 hour.

OVEN-EASY MEAT LOAF

350°

Oven time: 50–60 minutes

2 pounds ground beef
1 5-ounce can evaporated milk or ½ cup milk
2 packages dried onion soup mix

Mix all the ingredients together and form into a loaf in the Dutch oven. Bake.

This recipe is flexible and may be doubled or halved as needed.

STORING MEATS

Different meats have different storage needs.
Here are some tips:

- **Steaks, chops, and roasts.** Remove the wrapper from these meats as soon as possible. Scrape or wipe the meat, and rewrap it with the package ends left open. Store in the coldest part of the refrigerator for no more than 2 or 3 days.
- **Ground meats.** Cook all ground meats within 24 hours of purchase.
- **Mildly smoked meats.** Ham, bacon, and other mildly smoked meats should be refrigerated at all times. Use them within 2 weeks of purchase.
- **Cooked meats.** Cover cooked meats as soon as the meal is over; they need not be completely cooled. Store in the refrigerator.

GROUND BEEF BALLS

350°

Oven time: 25–30 minutes

4 pounds ground beef, not too lean
2 tablespoons salt
1 teaspoon pepper
1 teaspoon cinnamon
½ cup Worcestershire sauce
1 teaspoon chili powder
6 drops hot sauce, such as Tabasco
1 cup water

1. Form the beef into balls the size of large walnuts and place in a Dutch oven.

2. Mix the spices with the water and pour over the meatballs.

3. Fill the oven half full with water and bake.

MINI MEAL SIRLOIN BALLS

350°

Oven time: Simmer 35–45 minutes

1 cup salt-free tomato juice
4 cups water
3 tablespoons margarine
2 pounds lean sirloin, ground
1 cup uncooked rice
1 tablespoon chopped onion
1½ tablespoons chopped parsley
½ tablespoon dill
2 egg whites
⅛ teaspoon pepper
Dash salt
1 cup flour

1. Place the tomato juice, water, and margarine in a Dutch oven bottom and bring to a boil.

2. Mix the sirloin with the rice, onion, parsley, dill, egg whites, pepper, and salt. Form into balls.

3. Roll the balls in flour and drop into the boiling tomato juice mixture.

4. Simmer, covered, until done.

ROUND STEAK AND POTATO PIE

250°–350°

Oven time: Simmer 1–1½ hours at 250°
Bake 30–45 minutes at 350°

2 pounds round steak, cut into 1-inch cubes
2 tablespoons cooking oil
1 package brown gravy mix
½ cup water
2 cups tomato sauce or cut-up tomatoes
1 cup diced celery
1 medium onion, diced
4 medium potatoes, cooked, peeled, and cut into slices
¼ cup melted margarine
¼ cup grated Parmesan cheese
1 tablespoon minced chives

1. Brown the steak in the oil. Drain.

2. Add the gravy mix, stirring in the water and tomato sauce or cut-up tomatoes.

3. Place the cover on the Dutch oven, using just enough charcoal under and on top to simmer 60 minutes.

4. Add the celery and onion.

5. Continue to simmer until the meat is tender.

6. Place the cooked potatoes on top of the mixture.

7. Stir together the margarine, Parmesan, and chives. Sprinkle this mixture over the top and bake.

BEEF ROUND

325°

Oven time: 70–80 minutes

3 pounds round steak
1 cup flour
2 cups milk
1 egg, beaten
1 teaspoon salt
¼ teaspoon pepper

1. Cut the steak into 1-inch cubes and place in a Dutch oven.

2. Make a batter by mixing the flour, milk, beaten egg, salt, and pepper.

3. Pour the batter over the steak and bake until the meat is tender.

BEEF-BEAN OVEN DISH

350°

Oven time: 40–50 minutes

2 pounds ground beef
1 medium onion
1 small green pepper, chopped
1 cup chopped celery
3 tablespoons Worcestershire sauce
1 cup catsup
3 tablespoons brown sugar
1 28-ounce can pork and beans

1. Brown the beef in an open Dutch oven along with the onion, pepper, and celery.

2. Add the remaining ingredients, mix well, and bake.

BEEF MAIN DISH

350°

Oven time: 1¼–1½ hours

2 pounds ground beef, not too lean
4 large carrots
4 medium onions
4 large potatoes
Salt and pepper

1. Divide the ground beef into four balls or patties, salted and peppered as you like.

2. Place in a Dutch oven.

3. Quarter the carrots or cut into ½-inch slices.

4. Peel and quarter the onions.

5. Cut the potatoes in ½-inch slices or cube into 1-inch pieces.

6. Place all the vegetables in the Dutch oven on top of and around the meat, salting as desired.

7. Bake until the vegetables and meat are done.

SUGGESTED MENU

Beef Main Dish
Cranberry juice
Rolls
Lettuce wedges
Apples

BEEF-MACARONI CHEESIT

300°

Oven time: 20–30 minutes

1 pound ground beef
2 tablespoons diced onion
2 tablespoons margarine
2½ cups water
1 teaspoon salt
¼ teaspoon pepper
1 7- or 8-ounce box elbow macaroni
1 10¾-ounce can cream of mushroom soup
¼ pound diced sharp cheese
½ cup milk

1. Brown the beef and diced onion with the margarine in the bottom of a Dutch oven.

2. Remove the beef and onion mixture to an extra pan.

3. Place 2½ cups water in the Dutch oven, adding the salt and pepper.

4. Bring to a boil, add the macaroni, cover, and let cook until there is very little water in bottom, stirring two or three times during the cooking to keep the macaroni broken apart.

5. Stir in the browned beef and onion mixture. Add the mushroom soup, diced cheese, and milk, and bake at 300°.

6. As the dish bakes, do not add too much charcoal at one time, to prevent curdling.

Variation: Use 1 package macaroni and cheese dinner, following the directions on the package.

BEEF-NOODLE OVEN DISH

350°

Oven time: 30–40 minutes

1 pound ground beef
1 medium onion, chopped
1 medium green pepper, chopped
1 garlic clove, chopped
1 16-ounce package egg noodles, cooked as directed
    on package
1 10¾-ounce can mushroom soup
1 10¾-ounce can tomato soup
1 15-ounce can whole-kernel corn
1 cup grated or chopped sharp cheese

1. Brown the ground beef.

2. Add the onion, green pepper, and garlic.

3. Cook the noodles in an open Dutch oven until tender, and drain.

4. Add all ingredients except the cheese. Mix well.

5. Sprinkle cheese on top and bake.

SUGGESTED MENU

Beef-Noodle Oven Dish
Grapefruit juice
Spinach
Rye bread
White cake

BEEF-TOMATO-POTATO ONE POT

350°

Oven time: 35–50 minutes

4 medium potatoes
1 large onion
1 medium green pepper
2 pounds lean ground beef
1 10¾-ounce can tomato soup
Salt and pepper

1. Peel and cut the potatoes into 1-inch cubes.

2. Chop the onion and green pepper.

3. Add all the ingredients to a Dutch oven and bake for 35 to 50 minutes. Test the potatoes for doneness by sticking them with a fork.

CHILI

350°

Oven time: 45 minutes

1½ pounds ground beef, browned and drained
1 small onion, diced
1 teaspoon salt
½ teaspoon pepper
2 15-ounce cans tomatoes
1 tablespoon chili powder
1 14-ounce can spaghetti sauce
1 15-ounce can kidney beans
1 cup water
1 tablespoon sugar

1. Brown the beef with the onion, salt, and pepper. Drain.

2. Add the remaining ingredients and bake.

KIDNEY BEANS WITH BEEF

350°

Oven time: 35–40 minutes

1 pound ground beef
1 8-ounce can tomato sauce
1 medium onion, chopped
1 teaspoon salt
¼ teaspoon garlic salt
1 15-ounce can red kidney beans
2½ cups corn chips
1 cup shredded sharp cheese

1. Brown the ground beef. Set aside.

2. Blend the tomato sauce, onion, salt, garlic salt, and beans. Mix well.

3. Line bottom of a Dutch oven with corn chips, saving ½ cup.

4. Pour the beef over the chips, then spread the bean mixture over the beef.

5. Bake 30 to 35 minutes.

6. Sprinkle the shredded cheese and remaining crushed corn chips over the top. Bake 5 minutes more.

MEASURING TIP

Measuring exactly will assure you of something more than failure.

MEAT AND POTATO CASSEROLE

350°

Oven time: 30 minutes

¾ to 1 pound lean ground beef or turkey
½ cup chopped onion
3 cups (10 ounces) frozen shredded potatoes, thawed
2 cups (16-ounce can) sliced carrots, drained
1¾ cups (15-ounce can) chunky tomato sauce
⅛ teaspoon lemon pepper
1 teaspoon dried basil
1 cup frozen peas, thawed
¾ cup (3 ounces) reduced-fat Cheddar cheese

1. Brown the meat and onion together.

2. Add all the remaining ingredients.

3. Place in a Dutch oven and bake.

OVEN HASH

350°

Oven time: Preheat bottom of Dutch oven 15 minutes
Bake 20–30 minutes

2 cups cooked beef, cubed
2 cups cooked potatoes, cubed
1 large onion, chopped
Salt and pepper
¼ cup cooking oil
½ cup water

1. Pour the beef, potatoes, and onion into a Dutch oven, adding salt and pepper and stirring in the cooking oil.

2. Brown 10 to 15 minutes in an open oven, stirring occasionally.

3. Add the water to the mixture and stir.

4. Cover the oven and bake 20 to 30 minutes.

SUGGESTED MENU

Oven Hash
Cranberry juice
Pickled beets
White bread
Fresh pineapple

VEAL STEW WITH NOODLES

350°–300°

Oven time: Simmer 1¼ hours

2 pounds breast or neck of veal
¼ cup flour
2 tablespoons cooking oil
1 tablespoon vinegar
⅛ teaspoon pepper
6 medium onions, quartered
1 cup wide noodles (non-egg preferred)
1 cup sliced celery
1 tablespoon paprika
1 tablespoon chopped parsley

1. Cut the veal into six pieces, roll in flour, and brown in cooking oil in a Dutch oven bottom.

2. Sprinkle with vinegar and pepper, cover with cold water, and bring to a boil.

3. Reduce the coals, cover the oven, and simmer for 45 minutes.

4. Add the onions, noodles, and celery, simmering for 30 minutes more.

5. Serve hot, garnished with paprika and parsley.

PORK-BEEF SHISH

350°

Oven time: 1–1¼ hours

Skewers
1½ pounds sirloin, trimmed and cubed
1½ pounds pork chops, trimmed and cubed
1 teaspoon salt substitute
1 cup bread crumbs
¼ cup canola oil
1 16-ounce can whole tomatoes, drained
1 celery rib, diced
2 medium onions, diced
2 carrots, diced
½ cup water

1. Place alternating pieces of pork and beef on the skewers. Roll in a mixture of the bread crumbs and salt substitute.

2. Brown the skewered meat in the cooking oil in a Dutch oven bottom.

3. Pour the tomatoes, celery, onions, and carrots over the meat. Add the water and cook until tender.

BBQ PORK CHOPS DUTCH OVEN STYLE

350°

Oven time: 1¼–1½ hours

6 pork chops
1 tablespoon cooking oil
Salt and pepper
¾ cup catsup
1 8-ounce cola drink

1. Brown the chops in the cooking oil in a Dutch oven bottom.

2. Mix the catsup and cola with salt and pepper and pour into the oven over the chops.

3. Bake until the chops are done.

PREHEATING TIP

Start preheating your Dutch oven to the correct temperature before you start mixing the recipe.

PORK CHOP BAKE
350°
Oven time: 45–55 minutes

6 pork loin chops, ½ inch thick
1 tablespoon margarine
½ cup chopped onion
1¼ cup instant rice
1¼ cup water
1 cup diced tart apple (with or without peel)
1 peeled and diced orange
⅛ teaspoon black pepper
⅛ teaspoon savory
⅛ teaspoon cumin

1. Trim all the fat you can from the chops. Brown them quickly in margarine using a Dutch oven lid.

2. Sauté the onion in the drippings.

3. Stir in the remaining ingredients and arrange the chops on top.

4. Cover the oven and bake until the chops are tender.

PORK CHOPS OLD-HOME STYLE

350°

Oven time: Preheat 15 minutes
Bake 50–60 minutes

6 pork chops
Salt and pepper
1 tablespoon cooking oil
3 tablespoons margarine
4 cups seasoned croutons
¼ cup water
3 medium potatoes, quartered, peeled or unpeeled
1 10¾-ounce can mushroom soup
½ cup water

1. Place the chops in a hot Dutch oven with the cooking oil, salt, and pepper.

2. Melt the margarine in the Dutch oven lid.

3. Mix the croutons with the margarine, adding ¼ cup of water.

4. Shape the croutons into small balls and lay on top of the chops.

5. Place the potato quarters around the chops.

6. Pour the mushroom soup over the top, add ½ cup of water, and bake.

SUGGESTED MENU

Pork Chops Old-Home Style
Celery soup
Green beans
Whole-wheat bread
Apple cobbler

MUSHROOMED PORK STEAK

300°

Oven time: 65–75 minutes

6 lean pork steaks
Salt and pepper
2 teaspoons cooking oil
½ cup chopped onion
1 13-ounce can mushrooms
1 16-ounce can beef broth
2 teaspoons Worcestershire sauce
1 cup condensed milk
1 teaspoon flour

1. Salt and pepper the steaks.

2. Brown in the cooking oil.

3. Add the chopped onion as the steaks are browning.

4. Drain the mushrooms, pouring the liquid over the steaks.

5. Add the beef broth and Worcestershire sauce.

6. Bake 50 to 60 minutes.

7. Add the mushrooms.

8. Combine the condensed milk and flour, pour over the steaks, and bake 15 minutes more.

COUNTRY-STYLE SPARE RIBS

350°

Oven time: 2½–3 hours

4–5 pounds country-style ribs
1 cup catsup
Dash pepper sauce
1 teaspoon chili powder
1 teaspoon salt
⅓ cup Worcestershire sauce
1 cup water

Place the ribs in a cold Dutch oven and cover with a sauce made from the remaining ingredients. Bake until well done.

KRAUT AND SPARE RIBS COUNTRY STYLE

350°

Oven time: 50–60 minutes

1 16-ounce can sauerkraut
1 teaspoon salt
⅛ teaspoon pepper
1 tablespoon brown sugar
3 pounds country-style spare ribs

1. Pour the sauerkraut into a Dutch oven.

2. Add the salt, pepper, and brown sugar.

3. Arrange the spare ribs on top of the kraut.

4. Bake until the ribs are good and done.

Extra touch: Add a chopped apple to the kraut before serving.

HAM AND POTATO BAKE

350°

Oven time: 30 minutes

15 ounces frozen shredded potatoes, thawed
1½ cup frozen peas, thawed
1 cup diced extra-lean ham
½ teaspoon parsley flakes
¼ teaspoon pepper
1 10¾-ounce can low-fat cream of mushroom soup

Combine all the ingredients, pour into a Dutch oven, and bake.

 ## HAM AND CORN BAKE

350°

Oven time: 35 minutes

2 cups (1 16-ounce can) whole-kernel corn, drained
¼ cup chopped green pepper
½ cup chopped onion
1½ cups (9 ounces) chopped extra-lean ham
1 10¾-ounce can low-fat cream of mushroom soup
1 teaspoon prepared mustard
1 teaspoon dried parsley flakes
1 cup (2 ounces) crushed Ritz reduced-fat crackers

1. Combine all the ingredients, except the crackers. Mix well.

2. Add the crushed crackers.

3. Pour into a Dutch oven and bake.

BACON BAKE

350°

Oven time: 40–50 minutes

2 pounds sliced bacon

1. Cut the bacon slices in half.

2. Place in the Dutch oven and cover.

3. Bake until done, stirring two or three times as needed.

4. Drain on paper towels.

BACON-BEAN OVEN DISH

350°

Oven time: 30–40 minutes

2 15-ounce cans pork and beans
½ cup brown sugar
2 tablespoons white sugar
1 small onion, chopped
1 small green pepper, chopped
1 tablespoon Worcestershire sauce
2 strips bacon, diced

1. Mix all ingredients except the bacon in a Dutch oven.

2. Sprinkle the bacon pieces on top and bake.

MEAL IN AN OVEN

300°

Oven time: 35–40 minutes

1 medium onion
2 medium green peppers
½ cup uncooked extra-long rice
16 Oscar Mayer Smokie Links
1 can (1 pound, 12-ounce) tomatoes

1. Cut the onion into slices and lay them in the bottom of a Dutch oven.

2. Cut the green pepper into 1-inch rings and lay on top of the onion.

3. Place 1 tablespoon of rice in each ring.

4. Place two Smokie Links on each ring.

5. Pour the tomatoes over the top and bake.

SAUSAGE ROLL

350°

Oven time: Preheat 15 minutes
Bake 20–30 minutes

2 cups baking mix
⅓ cup cornmeal
¾ cup milk
1 pound bulk sausage, browned and drained

1. Combine the baking mix, cornmeal, and milk; mix thoroughly to make a stiff batter.

2. Roll out into a long, oval shape, ¼ inch thick.

3. Cover the dough with a layer of sausage and roll up like a jelly roll.

4. Cut into thin slices; bake in a preheated Dutch oven until done.

SAUSAGE-CHEESE BALLS

350°

Oven time: Preheat 15 minutes
Bake 15–20 minutes

3 cups baking mix, such as Bisquick or Jiffy
1 pound sausage, browned and drained
1 pound sharp cheese, grated
2 tablespoons milk

1. Place all the ingredients in a pan and mix thoroughly.

2. Make into 1-inch balls and place in greased or sprayed Dutch oven to bake.

Variation: Using the same ingredients, flatten the balls to ¾ inch thick and place in the oven to bake.

SAUSAGE-CHEESE BISCUITS

400°

Oven time: 30–40 minutes

3 cups baking mix
1 pound ground sausage, browned and drained
1 pound sharp cheese, grated

1. Mix all the ingredients together.

2. Form into 1-inch balls and flatten to ¾ inch thick.

3. Lay in a Dutch oven in two layers. Bake.

SAUSAGE-RICE OVEN DISH

350°

Oven time: 30–40 minutes

2½ pounds ground sausage
1 medium green pepper, chopped
1 medium onion, chopped
1 cup chopped celery
2 cups cooked rice
3 packages dry chicken noodle soup mix
1 4-ounce jar pimentos, chopped
1 10¾-ounce can cream of chicken soup
1 package almonds, slivered

1. Brown the sausage and drain.

2. Add the green pepper, onion, and celery and simmer in an open Dutch oven for 15 minutes.

3. Add the cooked rice and dry soup mix.

4. Add the pimentos, cream of chicken soup, and almonds. Bake.

SUGGESTED MENU
Sausage-Rice Oven Dish
Tomato juice
Green beans with celery
Rye bread
Spice cake

EGG-DOG BAKE

350°

Oven time: Preheat 10 minutes
Bake 20–30 minutes

6 eggs
1½ cups milk
⅓ cup cooking oil
½ cup potato flakes
Salt and pepper
¼ cup finely diced onion
6 hot dogs

1. Mix the eggs, milk, cooking oil, potato flakes, salt, and pepper thoroughly.

2. Add the onion and bite-size pieces of hot dogs.

3. Pour into a hot oven and bake 10 to 20 minutes.

4. After it's firm you can turn this dish to brown it on all sides if you wish. To test for doneness, stick the dish with a fork to see whether its center is solid.

SAUERKRAUT AND HOT DOGS

350°

Oven time: 20–30 minutes

1 16-ounce can sauerkraut
1 tablespoon brown sugar
8 hot dogs

1. Pour the sauerkraut into a Dutch oven.

2. Add the brown sugar.

3. Lay the hot dogs on top of sauerkraut and bake.

Variation: Cooked sausages, thuringer, or smoked cooked chops may be used in place of the hot dogs.

HAVE FUN!
Be sure to let other people help
you with preparing meals.
That's where the fun is!

Poultry

BAKED CHICKEN

350°

Oven time: Preheat 15 minutes
Bake 30–40 minutes

4–5 medium chicken quarters
Salt and pepper
½ stick (¼ cup) margarine

1. Place the chicken in a Dutch oven, salt and pepper it, add the stick margarine in small dabs, and bake.

2. The chicken is done when the leg breaks from the thigh easily, or the white meat is tender.

SUGGESTED MENU

Baked Chicken

Split pea soup

Broccoli

Coleslaw

Corn muffins

Chocolate cake

CHICKEN BREASTS

350°

Oven time: 50–65 minutes

8 chicken breasts
1 3-ounce package dried beef slices
8 slices bacon
Salt and pepper
1 10¾-ounce can cream of mushroom soup
1 8-ounce carton sour cream

1. Bone the chicken breasts and roll one slice of bacon around each.

2. Place the dried beef slices in the bottom of a Dutch oven and lay the bacon-wrapped chicken breasts on top.

3. Salt and pepper to taste.

4. Combine the mushroom soup and sour cream. Pour over the breasts.

5. Bake until the chicken is tender.

BAKED CHICKEN BREASTS

375°

Oven time: 50–60 minutes

4 large chicken breasts
1 cup flour
½ teaspoon pepper
1 teaspoon Mrs. Dash seasoning
2 tablespoons paprika
½ teaspoon thyme
½ cup margarine
1 cup orange juice
1 tablespoon brown sugar
1 medium onion, diced

1. Prepare the breasts by removing the skin.

2. Mix the flour, pepper, Mrs. Dash, paprika, and thyme in a paper or plastic bag.

3. Place the chicken in the bag and shake, coating well.

4. Brown in ¼ cup of margarine in a Dutch oven bottom.

5. Combine the remaining ¼ cup of margarine with the rest of the ingredients and simmer in the oven lid for 4 or 5 minutes.

6. Pour over the browned chicken and bake until tender.

CHICKEN WITH TOMATO

350°

Oven time: 1–1½ hours

6 chicken breasts
1 teaspoon seasoned salt
Dash lemon pepper
1 15-ounce can whole tomatoes
1 medium onion
1 4-ounce can sliced mushrooms
⅛ teaspoon oregano
½ teaspoon celery seeds
1 garlic clove, minced

1. Skin and bone the chicken breasts and place in a Dutch oven. Add salt and pepper.

2. Cut the tomatoes into quarters, saving the juice, and place the quarters on top of the chicken.

3. Cut the onion into slices and place on top of the chicken.

4. Pour the liquid off the mushrooms and add the mushrooms to the oven.

5. Mix the oregano, celery seeds, and minced garlic in the tomato juice. Pour over the mixture in the oven.

6. Bake for 1 hour.

7. Open the oven and baste the chicken with the liquid around it.

8. Bake with the oven lid cracked another 10 minutes.

EASY CHICKEN CASSEROLE

350°

Oven time: 65 minutes

6 chicken breasts, skinned and boned, cut
   into 1-inch pieces
1 head broccoli, cut into florets
6 big mushrooms, sliced
1 red or green pepper, chopped
¼ cup chopped green onion
1 celery stick, chopped
1 cup shredded Cheddar cheese
1 10¾-ounce can cream of mushroom or
   cream of celery soup
1 cup mayonnaise
1 small can (about 3 ounces) onion rings, for topping

1. Mix all the ingredients (except the onion rings) together well in
a Dutch oven.

2. Cover and bake for 1 hour.

3. Open the lid and pour on the onion rings. Replace the lid.

4. Bake for 5 minutes more.

CHICKEN-VEGETABLE DISH

350°

Oven time: 15–20 minutes

1 teaspoon margarine
2 slices bread, crumbed
2 6-ounce cans boned chicken, or 2 cups cooked and
    diced chicken meat
1 10¾-ounce can cream of chicken soup
1 15-ounce can mixed vegetables
1 small onion, chopped fine

1. Melt the margarine and mix with half of the bread crumbs.

2. Combine all the ingredients except the remaining bread crumbs in a Dutch oven.

3. Spread the rest of the bread crumbs over the top and bake.

CLEAN AS YOU COOK

Here are a couple of quick tips:

- Wipe up as you go.
- Discard packaging as soon as you open it up.

TURKEY WINGS

350°

Oven time: 30 minutes per pound

1 stick (½ cup) margarine
2 tablespoons flour
4 plump turkey wings
Salt and pepper
½ cup water

1. Melt the margarine in a Dutch oven.

2. Sprinkle the flour over the margarine.

3. Lay the wings in the flour and margarine and turn to coat, adding salt and pepper.

4. Pour the water into the oven and bake until the wings are done, basting with juices every 10 to 15 minutes.

Variation: To brown the wings before baking, sear them in an open oven for 15 minutes.

TURKEY WITH MUSHROOMS

350°

Oven time: 30–40 minutes

1½ cups herb-seasoned croutons
2 6-ounce cans boned turkey or 3 cups cooked equivalent
1 4-ounce can mushrooms, whole or bits
1 15-ounce can chicken broth
2 tablespoons cold water
1 tablespoon flour
½ teaspoon salt

1. Spread the croutons in the bottom of a Dutch oven.

2. Place the turkey on the croutons.

3. Add the mushrooms with their juice.

4. Thicken the chicken broth in the Dutch oven lid by heating to a slow boil.

5. While the broth is heating, thoroughly mix the flour and the cold water in a cup with the salt.

6. Spoon 2 tablespoons of hot broth into the flour mixture, stirring until blended.

7. Add the flour mixture to the hot broth and blend by stirring thoroughly.

8. Pour over the turkey mixture and bake.

DUTCH OVEN PIZZA
400°
Oven time: 30–40 minutes

Topping

2 tablespoons polyunsaturated vegetable oil
2 pounds ground raw turkey
2 cups chopped onion
1 large garlic clove, minced
1 cup chopped green pepper
1 cup unsalted tomato paste
2 teaspoons pure chili powder
1 teaspoon oregano
¼ teaspoon pepper

1. Heat the oil and brown the turkey in it until done.

2. Add the onion, garlic, and green pepper. Cook until the onion is transparent.

3. Add the tomato paste, chili powder, oregano, and pepper.

Crust

1 cup unbleached flour
1 cup yellow cornmeal
1 tablespoon baking powder
3 tablespoons polyunsaturated oil
2 egg whites
1 cup skim milk

1. Stir the dry ingredients together. Add the oil, egg whites, and milk, stirring in lightly.

2. Spread the batter in the bottom of a lightly sprayed Dutch oven.

Pizza

1 batch topping
1 crust
1 cup grated part-skim or nonfat mozzarella cheese

1. Spoon the topping over the pizza crust in the Dutch oven bottom. Sprinkle with cheese.

2. Bake until the crust around the sides is well browned.

KEEP IT HOT

To keep cooked food hot to serve later, try one of these methods:

- Wrap several layers of newspaper around your Dutch oven and place the whole thing in an insulated ice chest.
- Remove all but two or three coals from beneath and atop your Dutch oven until you're ready to serve.

Fish

BAKED TROUT OR OTHER FISH

350°

Oven time: 30–40 minutes

4 pounds trout fillets
8 strips bacon
1 small onion, chopped
Salt and pepper

1. Place a layer of fillets skin-side down in the bottom of a greased Dutch oven.

2. Cross with strips of bacon, then repeat layers as necessary.

3. Sprinkle the chopped onion on top.

4. Add salt and pepper.

5. Bake until the fish flakes easily.

Variation: If desired, lemon or lime juice may be sprinkled on the fish before baking.

FRIED TROUT OR OTHER FISH

350°

Trout 8 to 10 inches long are tastiest when cooked fresh. Clean and salt the fish, and fry them in hot shortening or oil in a Dutch oven lid or bottom.

Variation: Before frying, dip the fish in cracker crumbs, cornmeal, or a prepared dip.

WOODY'S DUTCH OVEN BAJUN FLYING FISH

350°

Oven time: 20–30 minutes

12 ½-inch-thick fish fillets, cut to approximately 3 by 6
    inches (almost any kind of fish will bake fine)
2 limes or juice equivalent
2 medium onions
½ teaspoon salt
Pepper
1 tablespoon cooking oil
1 tablespoon beef bouillon granules or 1 cube
1 6-ounce can tomato paste
1 cup water
1 teaspoon salt
1 teaspoon oregano

1. Sprinkle the lime juice over the fillets and let stand 10 minutes.

2. Dice the onions fine, adding salt, pepper, and cooking oil.

3. Wash the lime juice from the fillets and blot with paper towels.

4. Sprinkle the onion mixture on each fillet and roll up skin-side out.

5. Place in a Dutch oven.

6. Heat the water and dissolve the bouillon in it.

7. Mix together the tomato paste, bouillon, salt, more pepper, and
   oregano and pour over the fillets.

8. Bake about 20 minutes and check for tenderness. The fish should
   flake when moved with a fork.

BAKED FISH WITH SALSA TOPPING

350°

Oven time: 30 minutes

4 pieces white fish (about 1 pound total)
Butter-flavored cooking spray
2 teaspoons parsley flakes
½ cup chunky salsa (mild, medium, or hot, as desired)
¼ cup fat-free sour cream

1. Place the fish in a Dutch oven.

2. Lightly spray them with butter-flavored cooking spray.

3. Sprinkle the parsley flakes over the top.

4. Bake, covered, for 20 minutes.

5. In a small bowl, mix the salsa and sour cream.

6. Open the Dutch oven and evenly spoon the mixture over the fish.

7. Bake 10 minutes more or until the fish flakes easily.

SALMON LOAF
350°
Oven time: 50–60 minutes

1 14¾-ounce can pink or red salmon
1 egg
1 cup bread crumbs
¼ teaspoon onion powder
¼ teaspoon garlic powder
¼ teaspoon celery seed
Dash salt

1. Mix all ingredients well.

2. Form into a loaf, place in a Dutch oven, and bake until done.

TUNA SPAGHETTI DISH

350°

Oven time: 40–50 minutes

1½ cups broken spaghetti
1 small onion, chopped
¼ green pepper, chopped
1 10¾-ounce can cream of mushroom soup
1 6½-ounce can tuna, drained
½ pound cheddar cheese, diced
½ teaspoon salt

1. Cook the spaghetti in a Dutch oven and drain.
2. Combine the other ingredients with the spaghetti and bake.

SUGGESTED MENU

Tuna Spaghetti Dish
Vegetable juice
Coleslaw
Hot rolls
Ice cream

TUNA-NOODLE OVEN DISH

350°

Oven time: 35–45 minutes

2 6½-ounce cans tuna
1 10¾-ounce can cream of mushroom soup
½ cup almonds, slivered
1 6-ounce package egg noodles, cooked and drained
½ cup grated Colby or American cheese

1. Stir together the tuna, soup, and almonds.

2. Pour half of the noodles into the Dutch oven.

3. Add half of the tuna mixture.

4. Pour in remaining noodles and tuna.

5. Sprinkle grated cheese on top.

6. Bake 20 to 30 minutes, covered.

7. Crack open the lid of the oven and bake 15 minutes more, until light brown.

Wild Game

HOW TO PREPARE WILD GAME BIRDS

Cooking times for wild game birds vary, but with a little extra watching you can prepare them with that delicious flavor left in them.

If a bird is exceptionally old looking, properly clean and then boil it for half an hour. Then prepare according to the following recipe.

PHEASANT, PARTRIDGE, OR QUAIL

350°

Oven time: 20–30 minutes for pheasant or partridge
30–40 minutes for quail

1. Heat 2 cups water in a Dutch oven to boiling.

2. Split the birds in half and dip quickly in the hot water.

3. Add salt and pepper, and dust with flour.

4. Pour the water out of the oven and place halves meaty side up in oven.

5. Place a pat of margarine on each half.

6. Add 1 cup water after the first 10 minutes and baste every 10 minutes from then on until bird is done or the wings break off easily.

ROAST STUFFED DUCK

450°–350°

Oven time: Preheat 15 minutes
Bake 20 minutes per pound

1 4–5 pound roasting duck
2 teaspoons salt
¼ teaspoon pepper
2 cups Stuffing (see recipe below)

1. Prepare the duck for roasting by wiping the outside with a damp cloth. Salt and pepper it.

2. Stuff and tie the wings and legs closely to the body.

3. Place in a preheated Dutch oven, breast-side up.

4. Bake 15 minutes in 450° oven, then reduce the heat to 350° and bake 20 minutes per pound, being sure bird is done.

5. Baste every 10 to 15 minutes, starting by pouring 1 cup hot water over the duck after its first 15 minutes of searing, then using the juices from the oven for basting.

Stuffing
2 cups seasoned stuffing croutons
½ cup peanuts
2 tablespoons margarine
½ cup water
½ teaspoon onion juice

1. Crush the croutons into crumbs, chop the peanuts, and melt the margarine in the water.

2. Mix the croutons, peanuts, and onion juice with the margarine and water thoroughly.

DUTCH-OVEN-FRIED VENISON

350°

Oven time: 30–40 minutes

3 tablespoons cooking oil
Dash hot sauce
2 tablespoons Worcestershire sauce
Salt and pepper
2 pounds venison steaks

1. Heat the oil, hot sauce, and Worcestershire sauce in an oven.

2. Salt and pepper the steaks and fry until brown, then turn and brown the other side.

3. Cover the oven and bake. Serve hot.

Variation: Beef or pork steaks may be cooked in the same way, using the same sauce ingredients.

GET OUT OF THE RUT!
Try at least one new dish each day. Aim for well-balanced meals.

BAKED COON

350°

Oven time: 1–1¼ hours

For many wild meats, it's most important that you remove the musk glands and all hair. Coons have two glands under the front armpits. They appear as small, whitish, fatty, roundish lumps. They are very bitter and will ruin the taste of the meat if left in.

Remove all the fat possible before cooking.

To remove some of the wild flavor, if you wish, parboil the meat 20 to 30 minutes, adding 1 teaspoon salt. Pour off and add fresh water and salt. Repeat two or three times. Add 1 teaspoon vinegar to the final boiling.

1. When you're prepared to bake, place the meat on a rack in a Dutch oven in pieces.

2. Pour 2 cups water into the oven.

3. Add salt and pepper to taste.

4. Check in 15 to 20 minutes, adding more water if the meat is dry; wild game has a tendency to dry out while baking.

SUGGESTED MENU
Baked Coon
Candied yams
Fresh peas
Biscuits
Baked apple dumplings

HOW TO PREPARE RABBIT OR SQUIRREL

Get started with wild game and you will be glad you did—it's great and different if properly prepared. Domestic rabbit will be more tender and usually more meaty than wild rabbit. Both, if baked in a Dutch oven slowly, will produce a choice, tender morsel.

Prepare rabbit or squirrel by soaking overnight (in the refrigerator) in either salt water or ½ cup vinegar plus 2 cups water. A second choice is to pour boiling salt water over the meat and let stand 10 minutes, then pour the water off and finish baking.

Since wild game has a tendency to be dry, keep the meat covered with water at all times as it bakes.

WILD RABBIT OR SQUIRREL
(or Domestic Rabbit)

325°–350°

Oven time: 50–75 minutes

1 rabbit or squirrel, whole or cut into pieces
1 teaspoon salt
½ teaspoon pepper
1 medium onion, chopped
1 tablespoon vinegar
1 tablespoon margarine
Water to cover meat

1. Place the meat in a Dutch oven and add the salt, pepper, onion, and vinegar.

2. Dot with margarine.

3. Cover with water and bake until tender.

Vegetables

Legumes

BAKED MIXED VEGETABLES

350°

Oven time: 50–60 minutes

15-ounce package dried* lima beans
2 large carrots
2 medium onions
1 stick (½ cup) margarine
Salt and pepper
1 cup water

1. Soak the lima beans at least 1 hour before cooking.

2. Wash, scrape, and cut the carrots into slices.

3. Wash and slice the onions.

4. Place the beans, carrots, and onions by layers in a Dutch oven.

5. Dot each layer with margarine, salt, and pepper.

6. Pour in the water and bake until done.

* Frozen or fresh limas may be substituted for dried beans.

 **ASPARAGUS-PEA BAKE**

375°

Oven time: 15–25 minutes

1 tablespoon margarine
3 cups bread cubes, diced small and toasted brown in oven
1 16-ounce can small peas, drained
1 16-ounce can asparagus, drained, or 2 cups fresh
1 medium onion, chopped
2 tablespoons chopped pimentos
1 cup button mushrooms
1 cup 1 percent milk
⅛ teaspoon pepper
⅛ teaspoon salt

1. Melt the margarine in a Dutch oven bottom.

2. Place 1 cup of the bread cubes in the oven. Add half of the peas, asparagus, onion, pimentos, and mushrooms.

3. Top with another cup of bread cubes, then with the remaining half of the vegetables. Finish with another layer of cubes.

4. Mix the milk, pepper, and salt and pour over everything in the oven. Bake until done.

ASPARAGUS-PEA OVEN DISH

350°

Oven time: 30–40 minutes

1 15-ounce can asparagus, drained
1 15-ounce can peas, drained
1 10¾-ounce can mushroom soup
3 hard-boiled eggs, diced
1 medium green pepper, chopped
1 6-ounce can onion rings

1. Layer half of all the ingredients (except the onion rings) in a Dutch oven.

2. Repeat, topping with onion rings. Bake.

BAKED ASPARAGUS

300°

Oven time: 20–30 minutes

2 pounds asparagus, cut in 1-inch pieces
¼ cup water
1 cup buttered bread crumbs
¼ cup sour cream

1. Place the asparagus in a Dutch oven with the water.

2. Cover with bread crumbs.

3. Top with sour cream.

4. Bake until the crumbs are brown and the asparagus is tender.

Variation: Add grated cheese when crumbs are brown and let it melt.

SUGGESTED MENU
Meat loaf
Baked Asparagus
Baby beets
Corn bread sticks
Spiced pears
Cookies

CREAMY CHEESE GREEN BEANS

400°–300°

Oven time: 25 minutes at 400°
5–10 minutes at 300°

2 15-ounce cans green beans, any style
Salt and pepper
1 10¾-ounce can celery soup
1 cup finely chopped mild cheese (optional)

1. Drain the beans and place them in a Dutch oven with salt and pepper.

2. Pour the soup over the beans.

3. Bake 25 minutes.

4. Remove half of the charcoal from on top of and underneath the oven.

5. Sprinkle chopped cheese over the ingredients.

6. Bake 5 to 10 minutes more until the cheese melts.

GREEN BEANS WITH BACON BITS

350°

Oven time: 20–30 minutes

6 slices bacon, fried crisp
2 15-ounce cans green beans
1 10¾-ounce can mushroom soup
½ teaspoon salt
¼ teaspoon pepper

1. Fry the bacon until crisp, drain, and break into bits.

2. Place green beans (with liquid), mushroom soup, salt, and pepper in a Dutch oven.

3. Add the bacon bits and stir. Bake.

GREEN BEANS WITH MUSHROOMS

350°

Oven time: 30–40 minutes

2 15-ounce cans green beans
1 small onion, chopped
¼ teaspoon celery salt
1 4-ounce can mushrooms
1 cup crushed seasoned croutons
1 tablespoon margarine, melted

1. Drain the green beans and pour into a Dutch oven.

2. Add the onion and celery salt.

3. Pour the mushrooms (with liquid) over the beans.

4. Mix the croutons with the melted margarine.

5. Pour over the top of the mixture and bake until the crumbs are brown.

GREEN BEANS, ONION STYLE

350°

Oven time: 30–40 minutes

2 15-ounce cans green beans, any style
1 10¾-ounce can cream of mushroom soup
1 cup chopped onion

Mix all ingredients in a Dutch oven and bake.

Variation: In place of chopped onion, try french-fried onions for a different taste.

SWEET-AND-SOUR BAKED GREEN BEANS

350°

Oven time: 30–40 minutes

2 tablespoons cooking oil
2 tablespoons flour
2 tablespoons brown sugar
¼ teaspoon salt
2 tablespoons vinegar
⅛ teaspoon cinnamon
2 15-ounce cans cut green beans

1. Heat the oil in a Dutch oven.

2. Stir in the flour.

3. Add the remaining ingredients, mix well, and bake until thickened.

TOMATO GREEN BEANS

350°

Oven time: 20–30 minutes

2 tablespoons margarine
1 small onion, chopped
1 15-ounce can cut green beans, drained
1 15-ounce can tomatoes, chopped
1 10¾-ounce can mushroom soup
1 teaspoon Worcestershire sauce

1. Melt the margarine in a heated Dutch oven bottom.

2. Sauté the onion until tender.

3. Stir in the beans, tomatoes, mushroom soup, and Worcestershire sauce.

4. Bake until heated through.

LIMA BEANS WITH BACON

350°

Oven time: 20–30 minutes

4 strips bacon, chopped
1 15-ounce can lima beans
1 small onion, diced
2 small carrots, diced
1 tablespoon butter or margarine
½ teaspoon salt
⅛ teaspoon pepper
½ cup water

1. Put all the ingredients into a Dutch oven. Bake.

2. When the carrots are tender, serve.

BEETS WITH TOMATOES

350°

Oven time: 20–30 minutes

1 15-ounce can beets, drained and diced
1 15-ounce can tomatoes, chopped
½ cup grated or diced cheese
Salt and pepper
2 cups bread crumbs
2 tablespoons bacon drippings

1. Place half the beets in a Dutch oven.

2. Add half the tomatoes.

3. Add half the cheese.

4. Repeat these three layers.

5. Season with salt and pepper.

6. Add bread crumbs on top.

7. Pour bacon drippings over everything and bake.

SUGGESTED MENU

Beef and macaroni
Beets with Tomatoes
Lettuce wedges
Soft rolls
Gingerbread

BROCCOLI BAKE

350°

Oven time: 35–45 minutes

1-pound package frozen chopped broccoli
1 10¾-ounce can cream of mushroom soup
1 cup shredded sharp Cheddar cheese
¼ cup mayonnaise-type salad dressing
¼ cup milk
1 egg, beaten
½ cup bread crumbs
1 tablespoon margarine, melted

1. Cook the broccoli as directed on the package. Drain.

2. Mix the mushroom soup, cheese, salad dressing, milk, and beaten egg.

3. Pour over the cooked broccoli in the Dutch oven.

4. Mix the melted margarine and bread crumbs.

5. Sprinkle over the top of the broccoli mixture and bake.

SUGGESTED MENU

Beef roast
Broccoli Bake
Boiled cubed potatoes
Celery-apple salad
Rye bread
Strawberry pie

BROCCOLI WITH RICE

350°

Oven time: 20–30 minutes

1 cup instant rice
1 1-pound package chopped broccoli
1 medium onion, chopped
1 cup chopped celery
2 tablespoons shortening
1 10¾-ounce can cream of mushroom soup
1 10¾-ounce can cream of chicken soup
1 5-ounce jar cheese spread, sharp or seasoned
1 tablespoon margarine

1. Cook the rice in an open oven.

2. Cook the broccoli separately in an open oven.

3. Mix all the ingredients, except the cheese spread, in a greased Dutch oven. Bake.

4. Add the cheese spread and continue baking until the cheese melts.

CHEESED BROCCOLI

350°

Oven time: 45–60 minutes

2 10-ounce boxes frozen broccoli, or fresh equivalent*
2 cups diced or grated Cheddar cheese, mild or sharp

1. Follow the directions on the package to cook the frozen broccoli in a Dutch oven.

2. Sprinkle cheese on top.

3. Remove half the coals from the top and bottom of the Dutch oven. Let the broccoli remain in the oven about 5 minutes for the cheese to melt.

* *When using fresh broccoli, cook in ½ cup water in a Dutch oven, then follow the remaining directions.*

BAKED GREEN PEPPERS AND CABBAGE

350°

Oven time: 15–20 minutes

2 teaspoons cooking oil
1 medium green pepper, chopped
1 medium cabbage head, chopped
1 small celery stalk, chopped
1 small onion, chopped
1 15-ounce can tomatoes, chopped, or 2 medium
    fresh tomatoes, chopped
1 teaspoon sugar
1 teaspoon salt
½ teaspoon pepper

1. Heat the oil in a Dutch oven.

2. Add the remaining ingredients, stir, and bake until tender.

EASY CABBAGE BAKE

350°

Oven time: 15–20 minutes

½ cup water
¼ teaspoon salt
2 teaspoons instant beef bouillon
1 medium cabbage head, quartered

1. Dissolve the beef bouillon and salt in the water. Bring to a boil.

2. Add the cabbage.

3. When the water is boiling again, bake 15 to 20 minutes.

BAKED CARROTS

350°

Oven time: 15–20 minutes

1 15-ounce can diced carrots
2 tablespoons butter or margarine
1 teaspoon sugar
1 small onion, chopped
Salt and pepper

Mix all the ingredients in a Dutch oven and bake.

BAKED CORN

350°

Oven time: 25–35 minutes

2 tablespoons margarine
2 tablespoons flour
1¼ cups milk
1 tablespoon sugar
2 15-ounce cans whole kernel corn
2 eggs, beaten well
Salt and pepper

1. Melt the margarine in a Dutch oven.

2. Add the flour and blend well.

3. Stir in the milk slowly and bring to a boil.

4. Stir in the sugar and corn.

5. Stir in the well-beaten eggs.

6. Add salt and pepper to taste, and bake.

# CORN AND BROCCOLI CASSEROLE

350°

Oven time: 40 minutes

1 16-ounce can cream-style corn
1 egg
2 teaspoons dried onion flakes
⅓ cup shredded reduced-fat Cheddar cheese
3 cups frozen chopped broccoli, thawed
10 Ritz reduced-fat crackers, crushed

1. Combine the corn, egg, onion flakes, and cheese.

2. Stir in the broccoli.

3. Pour into a Dutch oven.

4. Sprinkle cracker crumbs over the top and bake.

POPCORN

Preheat a 9- by 9-inch aluminum Dutch oven to 450° for 15 minutes. When it's ready, pour 3 tablespoons of cooking oil in the bottom. Add ⅓ cup of popcorn, cover, and cook until the popcorn stops popping. Remove the coals from the bottom and top of the Dutch oven, and shake the oven a couple of times. Serve hot with butter and salt to taste.

CORN POTATO CASSEROLE

350°

Oven time: 45 minutes

⅔ cup nonfat dry milk powder
½ cup water
1 16-ounce can cream-style corn
2 teaspoons dried onion flakes
1 teaspoon parsley flakes
¼ cup (2-ounce jar) diced pimentos
¼ teaspoon pepper
½ cup frozen whole-kernel corn
6 cups (15 ounces) frozen hash brown potatoes

1. Combine the milk powder and water.

2. Stir in the cream-style corn, onion flakes, parsley flakes, pimentos and pepper.

3. Add the frozen corn and potatoes.

4. Mix well.

5. Pour into a Dutch oven and bake.

CORN-ONION-PIMENTO BAKE

350°

Oven time: 40–50 minutes

2 eggs, beaten
2 cups milk
2 tablespoons flour
1 15-ounce can cream-style corn
2 tablespoons margarine
1 tablespoon chopped onion
1 tablespoon chopped pimentos
2 tablespoons sugar
1 teaspoon salt

1. Beat the eggs and milk together in a Dutch oven bottom.

2. Stir in the flour.

3. Stir in the corn, margarine, onion, pimentos, sugar, and salt, mixing well.

4. Bake slowly until a knife comes out clean.

SCALLOPED CORN

300°

Oven time: 30–40 minutes

2 15-ounce cans cream-style corn
2 cups crushed Saltine crackers
3 eggs, beaten lightly
1 teaspoon salt
3 cups milk

Stir all ingredients together in a Dutch oven and bake.

Variation: Chopped pimentos may be added for extra taste.

EGGPLANT WITH CHEESE

350°

Oven time: 20–30 minutes

1 medium eggplant
½ teaspoon salt
2 teaspoons margarine
½ cup seasoned croutons, crumbled
¼ cup milk
1 egg, beaten
½ cup grated Colby cheese

1. Peel and cube the eggplant, and boil it in a small amount of water with salt until tender.

2. Mix the margarine, croutons, milk, egg, and ¼ cup of the cheese. Stir in the cooked eggplant lightly.

3. Pour into a greased Dutch oven.

4. Place the remaining ¼ cup cheese on top and bake.

Variation: Bread or cracker crumbs may be substituted for the croutons; add 1 teaspoon salt and ¼ teaspoon pepper.

BAKED ONIONS

350°

Oven time: 30–40 minutes

½ stick (¼ cup) margarine
2 tablespoons flour
1 cup milk
1 teaspoon salt
½ teaspoon pepper
3 eggs
4 medium onions

1. Melt the margarine and stir in the flour.

2. Gradually stir in the milk with the salt and pepper.

3. Beat the eggs and blend into the flour mixture.

4. Slice the onions and pour into the mixture.

5. Bake until the mixture sets up.

SUGGESTED MENU

Hamburger steaks
Grapefruit-orange cup
French fries
Baked onions
Corn muffins
Jell-O

ONION-CHEESE BAKE

350°

Oven time: 30 minutes

1 10¾-ounce can cream of mushroom soup
1 cup shredded sharp cheese
1 cup cheese crackers, crushed
2 15-ounce cans onions, drained
Paprika

1. Mix the soup, half of the shredded cheese, and half of the crushed crackers. Pour over the onions in a Dutch oven.

2. Sprinkle the remaining cheese and crackers over the top.

3. Sprinkle with paprika and bake.

CHEESE-COVERED PEAS

300°

Oven time: 15–25 minutes

1 15-ounce can peas, or 2½ cups cooked fresh peas
2 tablespoons cooking oil
1 cup grated sharp cheese
¼ teaspoon salt
⅛ teaspoon pepper
2 cups flavored croutons

1. Mix all the ingredients except the croutons in a Dutch oven.

2. Bake slowly.

3. When you're ready to serve, stir in the croutons.

PEAS WITH MUSHROOMS

350°

Oven time: 15–20 minutes

2 tablespoons margarine
2 4-ounce cans sliced mushrooms, drained
¼ cup slivered almonds
1 15-ounce can peas
1 10¾-ounce can mushroom soup
⅓ cup milk
1 4-ounce can pimentos, chopped

1. Sauté the mushrooms and almonds in the margarine in the bottom of a Dutch oven until the almonds are light brown.

2. Add the peas, mushroom soup, milk, and pimentos to the sautéed mushrooms and almonds.

3. Stir well, heating until bubbly.

BAKED POTATO SLICES

350°

Oven time: 35–50 minutes

4–5 medium potatoes
½ stick (¼ cup) butter or margarine
Salt and pepper

1. Wash the potatoes thoroughly and cut (with the skins on) into ½-inch slices.

2. Warm a Dutch oven and spread the bottom with a layer of margarine or butter and salt.

3. Spread slices of potatoes over the bottom, piling them up if necessary, and salting and peppering as the layers are added.

4. Place the remaining butter or margarine on the top layer with salt and pepper.

5. Bake until done.

BAKED POTATOES

350°

Oven time: 1–1¼ hours

4–5 large baking potatoes
Margarine

1. Place the potatoes in a Dutch oven.

2. Cut a cross in the top of each potato.

3. Place a dab of margarine on each cross.

4. Cover the oven and bake.

DUTCH OVEN FRIES

350°

Oven time: 30–40 minutes

⅛ teaspoon pepper
1 teaspoon vinegar
1 tablespoon cooking oil
1 tablespoon water
6 medium potatoes, peeled and cut into strips

1. Mix the pepper, vinegar, cooking oil, and water in a Dutch oven bottom.

2. Add the potatoes, cover the oven, and bake until done.

SCALLOPED POTATOES

300°

Oven time: 1¼–1½ hours

4 cups thinly sliced potatoes
Salt and pepper
1 tablespoon minced onion or several slices
¼ stick (2 tablespoons) margarine
1¼ cups milk

1. Place the thinly sliced potatoes in a Dutch oven.

2. Add salt and pepper.

3. Add the minced or sliced onion.

4. Place dabs of margarine on top.

5. Add the milk.

6. Bake until the potatoes are done.

SUGGESTED MENU

Swiss steak
Scalloped Potatoes
Buttered asparagus
Jellied vegetables
Peach pie

SPINACH DELUXE

350°

Oven time: 30–40 minutes

2 10-ounce packages frozen spinach, or
  2 15-ounce cans spinach
½ cup seasoned croutons
1 10¾-ounce can cream of onion soup

1. If you're using frozen spinach, cook it in boiling water for 10 minutes and drain. With canned spinach, discard the water and pour the contents into a Dutch oven.

2. Crush the croutons over the spinach. Pour the onion soup on top.

3. Bake until the dish turns light brown on top.

BAKED SQUASH

350°

Oven time: 35–50 minutes

2 8-inch-long and 2-inch-diameter zucchini squash
2 slices bacon, chopped
1 small onion, chopped
1 15-ounce can whole tomatoes or fresh tomato equivalent
Salt and pepper

1. Cut the squash in half lengthwise and remove the seeds.

2. Place in a Dutch oven cut-side up.

3. Sprinkle the chopped bacon, chopped onion, and tomatoes in the squash hollows. Add salt and pepper.

4. Bake until done.

SQUASH-CHEESE

350°

Oven time: 30–40 minutes

1 large acorn squash
1 cup water
1 medium onion, chopped
2 tablespoons margarine, melted
½ cup milk
1 egg
1 cup shredded sharp cheese
1 teaspoon salt
½ teaspoon pepper
1 cup cornflakes, crushed

1. Wash, peel, and cut the squash into 1-inch cubes.

2. Place in a Dutch oven with the water and bake 20 minutes.

3. Drain off the water and mash the squash, adding the onion, melted margarine, milk, egg, cheese, salt, and pepper.

4. Cover the top with crushed cornflakes and bake.

BAKED SWEET POTATOES

350°

Oven time: 40–50 minutes

4–6 medium sweet potatoes
2 tablespoons cooking oil
½ stick (¼ cup) margarine

1. Scrub the sweet potatoes and dry them.

2. Brush cooking oil on each and place in a Dutch oven.

3. Cut a cross in each about 1 inch long and lay a pat of margarine on top of each.

4. Bake until done.

SWEET POTATO CASSEROLE

350°

Oven time: 40–50 minutes

Casserole

1 2-pound, 8-ounce can sweet potatoes
1 stick (½ cup) margarine
1 teaspoon vanilla
1 cup brown sugar
⅓ cup canned evaporated milk
2 eggs
½ teaspoon cinnamon

1. Mash the sweet potatoes.
2. Melt the margarine and add to the potatoes.
3. Add the remaining ingredients and mix well.
4. Pour into a Dutch oven. Set aside.

Topping

½ stick (¼ cup) margarine
1 teaspoon vanilla
¾ cup brown sugar
½ cup flour
1 cup pecans, chopped fine
½ teaspoon cinnamon

1. Melt the margarine.
2. Add the remaining ingredients and mix. This topping will be thick and heavy.
3. Crumble over the top of the sweet potatoes.
4. Bake.

TANGY TOMATOES

400°

Oven time: 15–20 minutes

4 large fresh tomatoes
4 teaspoons prepared mustard
Salt and pepper
2 tablespoons margarine
½ green pepper, chopped
1 celery rib, chopped
2 green onions, chopped

1. Cut the tomatoes in half.

2. Place in a Dutch oven cut-side up.

3. Spread each with prepared mustard.

4. Salt and pepper each.

5. Melt the margarine; chop the pepper, celery, and onions. Add all to the top of the tomatoes.

6. Bake and serve.

PREPARING FREEZE-DRIED OR DEHYDRATED TRAIL FOODS

You can cook any of the commercially available packaged trail foods in your Dutch oven. Simply follow the directions listed on the package.

KIDNEY BEAN BAKE

350°

Oven time: 40–50 minutes

1 small onion, chopped
½ 4-ounce jar pimentos
⅓ cup catsup
1 16-ounce can kidney beans
4 strips bacon

1. Mix the onions, pimentos, catsup, and beans in a Dutch oven.

2. Lay the bacon on top of the mixture and bake.

Variation: Substitute canned beans in almost any style for the kidney beans.

REAL HAWAIIAN BEANS

350°

Oven time: 30–40 minutes

1 28-ounce can baked beans with pork and molasses
2 tablespoons brown sugar
Dash salt
½ teaspoon dry mustard
1 8-ounce can pineapple chunks, drained
    (reserve 4 tablespoons juice)
4 slices bacon

1. Pour the beans into a Dutch oven.

2. Add the brown sugar, salt, mustard, and pineapple chunks. Stir.

3. Lay strips of bacon on top.

4. Pour 4 tablespoons pineapple juice over the mixture and bake.

SIMPLE BAKED BEAN DISH

350°

Oven time: 30–40 minutes

1 28-ounce can pork and beans
1 8-ounce can tomato sauce
1 small onion, chopped
Salt and pepper

1. Mix all the ingredients in a Dutch oven and bake.

2. Serve with catsup and slices of onion on top.

Variation: Add a cup grated cheese, chopped almonds, or chopped walnuts before serving.

TEXAS BEANS

350°

Oven time: 30–45 minutes

½ pound bacon, diced
4 large onions, cut into rings
Dash garlic powder
¼ teaspoon dry mustard
½ cup vinegar
¾ cup dark brown sugar
1 8-ounce can lima beans, drained
1 16-ounce can kidney beans, drained
1 28-ounce can pork and beans

1. Fry the bacon in a Dutch oven bottom and add the onion rings.

2. Cook slowly until the onion rings are transparent.

3. Add the garlic, mustard, vinegar, and sugar.

4. Cook for 20 minutes, then add the beans.

5. Cover the oven, bake, and serve.

Eggs, Cheese, and Dairy

BOILED EGGS

1. Place eggs in a Dutch oven.

2. Pour in enough water to fill to ½ inch from the top.

3. Let the water come to a boil, then reduce the heat to a simmer for 7 to 8 minutes.

4. For soft-boiled eggs, reduce the cooking time to 2 or 3 minutes.

Variation: Follow steps 1 and 2; for step 3, bring the water to a boil, then cover and remove from the heat. The eggs will be soft boiled in about 5 to 10 minutes, hard boiled in about 20 to 25 minutes.

DEVILED EGGS

12 hard-boiled eggs
1 teaspoon salt
¼ teaspoon pepper
1 teaspoon mustard
6 tablespoons salad dressing, or lemon juice or vinegar
    to taste

1. Cut the hard-boiled eggs in half lengthwise and remove the yolks to a bowl.

2. Mash the yolks with a fork.

3. Add the remaining ingredients and mix well.

4. Fill the egg whites with mixture and serve.

Variation: Paprika may be sprinkled on top for color. A very small red pepper may be dotted on top of each, if you like hot foods.

DUTCH OVEN QUICHE
350°
Oven time: Preheat 10 minutes
Bake 30–40 minutes

4 slices bread
2 medium tomatoes, peeled and cubed
2 cups grated fat-free Swiss cheese
1 cup skim milk
½ cup egg substitute
½ teaspoon salt substitute
⅛ teaspoon pepper
1 teaspoon prepared mustard
1 pinch cayenne pepper

1. Cut the bread into cubes and arrange on the bottom of a sprayed Dutch oven.

2. Place the tomatoes over the bread and sprinkle with cheese.

3. Mix the milk, egg substitute, salt, pepper, mustard, and cayenne pepper. Pour over everything in the oven.

4. Bake until done and serve at once.

Variation: You can substitute any number of ingredients here, such as different types of low-fat cheeses, low-fat ham, mushrooms, onions, and more. Or try adding chopped broccoli to the recipe above for an extra vegetable taste.

CHEESE AND APPLE GRILL

400°

Oven time: Preheat 10 minutes
Bake 15–20 minutes

8 slices bread
Margarine
16 thin slices low-cholesterol cheese
Herb seasoning
8 apple slices, ½ inch thick

1. Spread margarine on one side of all the slices of bread.

2. Place the spread side of the bread down in a preheated Dutch oven.

3. Sprinkle on herb seasoning as desired. Put two slices of cheese on each bread slice. Top with one apple slice.

4. Place another slice of bread, spread-side up, on top of the apple slice.

5. Cover the oven. Bake one side for 10 minutes, then turn and continue baking until brown as desired.

MEASURING SHREDDED OR GRATED CHEESE

Pack the cheese lightly into a measuring cup until it's level with the top.

CHEESE GRITS

350°

Oven time: 30–45 minutes

4 cups water
1 cup grits
1 stick (½ cup) margarine
1 garlic clove, chopped
½ teaspoon salt
1 pound sharp cheese, diced
2 eggs, beaten lightly
½ cup milk

1. Bring the water to a boil in a Dutch oven.

2. Stir in the grits. Add the margarine, garlic, salt, and cheese.

3. Blend the eggs and milk; stir into the grits mixture in the oven and bake.

CHEESE NOODLE OVEN DISH

350°

Oven time: 20–30 minutes

1 7- or 8-ounce package noodles, cooked as directed
   on package
1 pound ground beef (optional)
1 medium onion, chopped
1 tablespoon margarine
1 teaspoon salt
¼ teaspoon garlic salt
⅛ teaspoon pepper
2 8-ounce cans tomato sauce
1 cup cottage cheese
1 cup sour cream
1 cup shredded cheese

1. Drain the cooked noodles.

2. Brown the beef in the margarine with the onions.

3. Add the salt, garlic salt, pepper, and tomato sauce.

4. Layer the noodles, beef, cottage cheese, and sour cream in a
greased Dutch oven.

5. Top with shredded cheese and bake.

CHEESE-SPREAD MINI SANDWICHES

350°

Oven time: 15–20 minutes

2 5-ounce jars sharp cheese spread
¼ cup soft margarine
1 egg
6 slices bread

1. Mix together the cheese spread and margarine.

2. Beat the egg and add to the mixture, stirring well.

3. Place a layer of bread in a Dutch oven.

4. Spread with cheese mixture.

5. Repeat the layers, ending with the cheese mixture.

6. Bake.

7. Cut into small squares and serve with a toothpick in each.

MACARONI AND CHEESE

300°

Oven time: 30–40 minutes

1 7-ounce box macaroni
½ pound cheddar cheese, sliced
2 cups milk
Salt and pepper

1. Bring 2 cups of water to a boil in a Dutch oven, adding 1 teaspoon of salt.

2. Add the macaroni to the water and let it come to a boil again, then stir.

3. Stir the macaroni two or three times while the water cooks down to ½ inch in the oven.

4. Put the cheese on top.

5. Pour in the milk, salt, and pepper. Bake.

6. Be sure the oven is only moderately hot; the milk will curdle if the heat is too high.

7. This dish is done when the milk has cooked down and the cheese is melted through.

SUGGESTED MENU

Beef roast
Macaroni and Cheese
Lettuce and tomato salad
Hard rolls
Sliced bananas

MUSHROOM MINI SANDWICHES

350°

Oven time: 20–30 minutes

2 tablespoons margarine, softened
6 tablespoons grated coconut
6 slices bread
1 10¾-ounce can cream of mushroom soup

1. Mix the softened margarine and coconut and spread a thin layer in the bottom of a Dutch oven.

2. Layer the bread over the margarine and coconut.

3. Spread the mushroom soup generously over the bread.

4. Repeat layers, ending with margarine coconut spread on top.

5. Bake 20 to 30 minutes or until browned.

6. Quarter the sandwiches with a sharp knife.

NOODLES ROMANOFF

300°

Oven time: 40–55 minutes

1 stick (½ cup) margarine
3 medium green peppers, chopped
2 packages dry onion soup mix
1 pound noodles, cooked
1 8-ounce carton sour cream
1 16-ounce carton small-curd cottage cheese

1. Cook the margarine, green peppers, and onion soup mix in an open oven for 15 minutes, stirring occasionally.

2. Mix the noodles and margarine mixture with the sour cream and cottage cheese. Bake.

Breads

EASY YEAST BREAD

450°

Oven time: 40–50 minutes

1½ cups milk
2 tablespoons sugar
¼ cup shortening
2 packages dry yeast
5½ cups flour
2 eggs
1½ teaspoons salt

1. Add the sugar and shortening to the milk and bring to a boil, stirring often.

2. Let cool to lukewarm.

3. Stir the yeast into the mixture.

4. Stir in 2 cups of the flour. Let rise until double—45 to 60 minutes at 75° to 80°.

5. Mix the eggs, remaining flour, and salt. Stir into the flour mixture, beating until smooth.

6. Place the dough in a greased Dutch oven and let rise until double.

7. Bake until the loaf is brown and sounds hollow when thumped.

Variations: To halve (or double) this recipe, simply halve (or double) the amount of each ingredient and bake in a Dutch oven that's as close to half size (or double size) as possible. The baking time should be approximately the same.

YEAST ROLLS OR BREAD

300°–375°

Oven time: 5 minutes at 300°
20–30 minutes at 375°

2 cups milk
¼ cup sugar
½ cup shortening
1 package yeast
4 cups flour
½ teaspoon salt
½ teaspoon baking soda
½ heaping teaspoon baking powder

1. Stir together the milk, sugar, and shortening in a pan. Bring to a boil.

2. Cool to lukewarm, then stir in the yeast.

3. Add 2 cups of the flour, stirring until smooth.

4. Let rise until doubled.

5. Stir in the remaining 2 cups of flour, salt, soda, and baking powder until smooth.*

6. Put the dough in a greased Dutch oven (either as rolls or in a loaf) and let rise until doubled.

7. Bake at 300° for 5 minutes.

8. Add coals to bring the Dutch oven to 375°, baking until the bread sounds hollow when thumped and is golden brown.

At this point the dough may be placed in the refrigerator overnight or for a few days, if you keep it punched down.

ANISE BREAD

350°

Oven time: 20–30 minutes

1 cup margarine or butter
½ cup sugar
6 eggs
4 drops anise oil
1½ tablespoons anise seeds
5 cups flour
4 teaspoons baking powder
¼ teaspoon salt

1. Cream the margarine or butter with the sugar and eggs.

2. Add the anise oil and seeds, and mix thoroughly.

3. Mix the flour, baking powder, and salt together and add to the creamed mixture.

4. Knead the dough—either in a mixing bowl or on a floured board—for 5 minutes.

5. Shape the dough into a loaf, place it in a greased Dutch oven, bake.

BATTER BREAD
400°
Oven time: 15–20 minutes

2 cups milk
2 tablespoons cornmeal
4 eggs

1. Heat the milk to warm, then add the cornmeal, stirring well.

2. Separate the egg yolks from the whites.

3. Beat the yolks and add to the mixture, mixing thoroughly.

4. Beat the egg whites until they stand up.

5. Fold lightly into the mixture.

6. Bake until brown.

"BIRD SEED"
Here's a simple between-meal snack recipe:
Just mix equal quantities of M&Ms,
peanuts, and raisins.

SPOON BREAD

350°

Oven time: 40–50 minutes

5 eggs
¼ cup white cornmeal
1 tablespoon sugar
½ teaspoon salt
2 cups milk
2 tablespoons margarine or butter, melted

1. Beat the eggs.

2. Stir in the cornmeal, sugar, salt, milk, and melted margarine.

3. Bake until the top is golden brown and puffed up.

SUGGESTED MENU

Broiled steak

Lima beans

Buttered broccoli

Spoon Bread

Fruit salad

BRAN LOAF

350°

Oven time: 25–35 minutes

2 cups All-Bran
2 cups flour
1 cup brown sugar
1 cup dates, chopped
2 teaspoons baking soda
2 cups buttermilk

1. Mix the bran, flour, brown sugar, and chopped dates.

2. In a separate bowl, mix the soda into the buttermilk.

3. Add the buttermilk mixture to the dry mixture and blend well.

4. Pour into a greased Dutch oven and bake until nice and brown.

BANANA NUT BREAD

375°

Oven time: Preheat 15 minutes
Bake 30–40 minutes

2½ cups flour
½ teaspoon baking soda
2 teaspoons baking powder
1 cup sugar
½ teaspoon salt
½ cup margarine
2 eggs
2 average bananas, ripe
½ cup buttermilk
1 teaspoon vanilla
1 cup pecans

1. Stir the flour together with the soda and baking powder.

2. In a separate bowl, cream the sugar and salt with the margarine. Add eggs and beat thoroughly.

3. In a third bowl, mash the bananas. Add the buttermilk and vanilla.

4. Add the flour mixture and bananas to the creamed mixture and beat well.

5. Stir in the pecans and bake until a toothpick comes out clean.

SOUR MILK OR BUTTERMILK SUBSTITUTE

*To replace 1 cup of sour milk or buttermilk,
put 1 teaspoon lemon juice or vinegar
in a measuring glass.
Add enough whole milk to fill to the cup line.*

DATE BREAD

350°

Oven time: 50 minutes

3½ cups flour
4½ teaspoons baking powder
1 teaspoon salt
½ cup sugar
1 egg, beaten
1 tablespoon cooking oil
1½ cups milk
1 cup chopped dates

1. Mix the flour, baking powder, salt, and sugar.

2. Add the beaten egg, oil, and milk to the dry mix and stir thoroughly.

3. Sprinkle a small amount of flour over the chopped dates and coat thoroughly. Stir into the mixture.

4. Place in a greased Dutch oven and let stand 20 minutes, then bake.

BROWN BREAD

400°

Oven time: 45–60 minutes

1 cup buttermilk
1 teaspoon baking soda
½ cup molasses (good sorghum works fine)
1 cup graham flour
1 cup cornmeal
½ teaspoon salt
¾ cup raisins
½ cup water

1. Mix the buttermilk and soda, adding the molasses.
2. In a separate bowl, mix the flour, cornmeal, and salt.
3. Add the liquid mixture to the flour mixture and blend well.
4. Add the raisins.
5. Place a rack in the Dutch oven.
6. Pour water in the bottom of the oven.
7. Make a shallow pan of aluminum foil and place it on the rack.
8. Place the dough on the foil pan and bake until it tests done with a toothpick and is well browned.

SUGGESTED MENU

Rolled beef roast

Rice

Spinach

Brown Bread

Applesauce

Coconut cake

FLUFFY MUFFIN ROLL LOAF

425°

Oven time: 20–30 minutes

1 cup milk
1 egg
¼ cup cooking oil
2 cups flour
3 teaspoons baking powder
3 tablespoons sugar
¼ teaspoon salt

1. Blend together the milk, egg, and cooking oil.

2. In a separate bowl, mix the flour, baking powder, sugar, and salt.

3. Lightly blend the two mixtures together.

4. Pour the batter into a greased Dutch oven and bake until brown.

QUICK BREAD

375°–425°

Oven time: 15–20 minutes

1 tablespoon margarine or butter, melted
1 loaf frozen pre-packaged bread dough, thawed

1. Grease a Dutch oven with a little cooking oil

2. Place the bread in the oven.

3. Brush margarine or butter over the top.

4. Bake until golden brown.

Variation: Poppy or sesame seeds may be added on top before baking, if desired.

MOLASSES BREAD
350°
Oven time: 1–1¼ hours

First Mix

1 cup white flour
2 cups whole-wheat flour
1 teaspoon salt
½ cup sugar

Second Mix

1½ teaspoons sugar
1½ cups milk
½ teaspoon baking soda
½ cup molasses

1. Thoroughly blend the first mix.

2. In a separate bowl, thoroughly blend the second mix.

3. Add the two mixes together and stir until smooth.

4. Pour into a greased Dutch oven and bake until a toothpick comes out clean.

MEASURING MOLASSES

Pour the liquid slowly into a measuring cup; it will mound up. Use a rubber scraper or flexible spatula to scrape it out of the cup.

PECAN BREAD

350°

Oven time: 50–60 minutes

3 cups flour
1 cup sugar
4 teaspoons baking powder
1 teaspoon salt
1 cup pecans, chopped
2 teaspoons lemon juice
3 eggs
1 cup milk
¼ cup cooking oil

1. Grease a Dutch oven.

2. Mix the flour, sugar, baking powder, and salt.

3. Stir in the pecans and lemon juice.

4. Beat the eggs with the milk. Add the oil. Pour into the flour mix and stir just until all is moist.

5. Pour into the Dutch oven and spread evenly.

6. Bake until a toothpick comes out clean. This bread stores well when wrapped in film wrap or aluminum foil.

ORANGE-NUT BREAD

400°

Oven time: 60–70 minutes

2½ cups flour
1 tablespoon baking powder
1½ teaspoons salt
1 cup walnuts, chopped
1 cup milk
2 eggs, beaten
½ cup orange marmalade
2 tablespoons cooking oil

1. Mix the flour, baking powder, salt, and nuts.

2. Add the milk and beaten eggs, stirring lightly.

3. Stir in the marmalade and oil.

4. Bake until brown.

SUGGESTED MENU

Baked chicken
Carrots
Orange-Nut Bread
Raspberry sherbet

RAISIN ROLLS

425°

Oven time: Preheat 15 minutes
Bake 20–30 minutes

2 cups flour
5 teaspoons baking powder
1 teaspoon salt
2 tablespoons sugar, divided
3 tablespoons shortening
⅔ cup milk
1 teaspoon margarine, melted
½ cup raisins
¼ cup pecans, chopped
½ teaspoon cinnamon

1. Mix the flour, baking powder, salt, and 1 tablespoon of the sugar.

2. Cut in the shortening with a knife or pastry cutter, or rub it in with your fingers.

3. Add the milk gradually and blend to a soft dough.

4. Roll out on a lightly floured board to ¼ inch thick.

5. Brush with melted margarine.

6. Sprinkle with the raisins, nuts, remaining 1 tablespoon sugar, and cinnamon.

7. Roll up like a jelly roll and cut into 1-inch slices.

8. Lay the slices flat in a greased Dutch oven and bake.

WARMING BREADS AND ROLLS

Place 4 tablespoons of water in the bottom of a Dutch oven, then put the bread or rolls on a rack. Heat in a very slow oven for 15 minutes until warmed.

SPICE-PEACH BREAD
350°
Oven time: 60–70 minutes

2 cups flour
⅔ cup sugar
2 teaspoons baking powder
½ teaspoon salt
½ teaspoon baking soda
¼ teaspoon ground cloves
2 tablespoons margarine, creamed or softened
2 cups peaches, sliced
½ cup water
2 eggs

1. Blend all ingredients at once until mixed thoroughly—approximately 2 minutes.

2. Pour into a greased and floured 6½- by 9-inch Dutch oven. Bake until a toothpick inserted in the center comes out clean.

Variation: Nuts, dates, or raisins may be added if desired—stir into the batter before pouring it into the oven.

BASIC BISCUIT MIX

8 cups flour
8 teaspoons baking powder
4 teaspoons salt
1 teaspoon sugar
1½ cups shortening

1. Mix the flour, baking powder, salt and sugar thoroughly.

2. Cut in the shortening with a pastry cutter, or mix with your hands to the texture of fine crumbs.

BISCUITS FROM BASIC MIX

475°

Oven time: Preheat 15 minutes
Bake 10–20 minutes

2 cups Basic Biscuit Mix
¾ cup milk

1. Add the milk to the mix slowly to make a soft dough.

2. Roll out and cut biscuits to ½ inch thick. Place in a preheated Dutch oven.

3. Bake until golden brown.

Variation: If desired, more milk may be added to the dough and the biscuits dropped by spoonfuls into a hot Dutch oven.

MEASURING WHITE (GRANULATED) SUGAR

Sift white sugar only if it's lumpy. Spoon it lightly into a dry measuring cup, then level off with a straightedge. Don't strike or tap the cup.

PEANUT BUTTER BISCUITS

375°

Oven time: 15–20 minutes

2 cups Basic Biscuit Mix or Jiffy baking mix
¾ cup milk
½ cup peanut butter
2 tablespoons cream
1 teaspoon sugar

1. Blend the mix and milk into a dough and roll or pat out to ¼ inch thick.

2. In a separate bowl, mix the peanut butter, cream, and sugar.

3. Spread this out on the dough.

4. Roll up like a jelly roll.

5. Cut into ¾-inch slices.

6. Place in a greased Dutch oven and bake until brown.

SUGGESTED MENU

Baked ham
Pineapple juice
Spanish rice
Peanut Butter Biscuits
Apples

BOILED ONION BISCUITS

Oven time: Boil in an open oven approximately 10 minutes

2 cups Basic Biscuit Mix
1 teaspoon salt
½ teaspoon pepper
¼ cup fine-chopped onion
⅔ cup milk

1. Bring water to a boil in a Dutch oven bottom.

2. Combine all the ingredients to a soft dough.

3. Turn the dough onto a surface dusted with flour and knead quickly twenty to twenty-five times.

4. Pat or roll out the dough ½ inch thick.

5. Cut with a floured cutter.

6. Place in boiling water and cook each biscuit until it looks done when you open it with a fork.

BROWN SUGAR CINNAMON BISCUITS

375°

Oven time: 15–20 minutes

2 cups Basic Biscuit Mix or Jiffy baking mix
¾ cup milk
¼ cup brown sugar
¼ cup white sugar
1 teaspoon cinnamon
1 tablespoon cooking oil or margarine, melted

1. Blend the mix and milk and roll or pat out ¼ inch thick.

2. Mix the brown and white sugars, cinnamon, and oil. Spread over the dough.

3. Roll like a jelly roll and cut into ¾-inch slices.

4. Place in a greased Dutch oven and bake until brown.

Variation: Nuts may be added, if desired.

WOODY'S DUTCH OVEN ORBIT BITS

425°

Oven time: 15–20 minutes

2 cups flour
1 tablespoon sugar
4 teaspoons baking powder
½ teaspoon salt
½ cup margarine or butter
1 egg
⅔ cup milk
¼ teaspoon seasoned salt, such as Lawry's
4 tablespoons grated Parmesan cheese

1. Mix the dry ingredients together.

2. Cut in the margarine or butter.

3. In a separate bowl, blend the egg and milk, then add to the flour mix and stir lightly until the dough follows your fork.

4. Lay on a board and knead gently twenty times.

5. Divide the dough in half.

6. Roll or pat out half the dough and place in a Dutch oven.

7. Mix the seasoned salt and Parmesan. Spread evenly over the dough.

8. Place the second half of the dough on top of the cheese mix.

9. Create bite-size pieces by cutting with a knife through both doughs to the size desired.

10. Bake until brown.

QUICK SPOON BISCUITS

375°

Oven time: 15–20 minutes

2 cups flour
½ cup salad dressing or mayonnaise
½ cup milk

1. Stir all the ingredients together well.

2. Drop by spoonfuls into a greased Dutch oven to the size desired.

3. Bake until golden brown.

HOT CHEESE BISCUITS

350°

Oven time: 10–15 minutes

½ pound Colby cheese, grated or chopped
2 sticks (1 cup) margarine, softened
2 cups flour
¼ teaspoon cayenne pepper
¼ teaspoon salt

1. Mix the grated cheese and margarine.

2. Add the flour, cayenne pepper, and salt. Mix well.

3. Roll out the dough on cloth or between pieces of wax paper.

4. Cut the biscuits and place in a Dutch oven.

5. Bake until golden brown.

CO

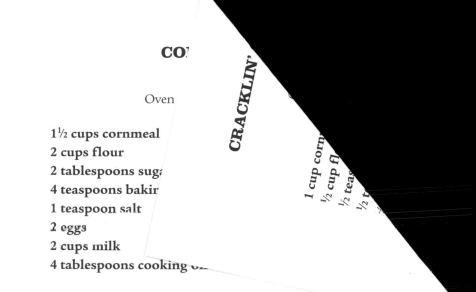

Oven

1½ cups cornmeal
2 cups flour
2 tablespoons sug;
4 teaspoons bakir
1 teaspoon salt
2 eggs
2 cups milk
4 tablespoons cooking oi

1. Mix the cornmeal, flour, sugar, baking powder, and salt in a Dutch oven.

2. Add the eggs and milk, stirring until smooth.

3. Stir in the oil or fat.

4. Bake until golden brown and serve hot right out of the oven. This bread is also good cold.

SUGGESTED MENU
Stuffed pork chops
Acorn squash
Coleslaw
Corn Bread
Apricots

GOOD CORN BREAD

350°

Oven time: 25–30 minutes

meal
ur
poon salt
aspoon sugar
teaspoon baking soda
2 teaspoons baking powder
1½ cups milk
1 tablespoon cooking oil
1 egg
½ cup cracklin's, crumbled

1. Mix together the cornmeal, flour, salt, sugar, soda, and baking powder.

2. In a Dutch oven lid, combine the milk, oil, egg, and cracklin's. Add this to the dry mix and beat well.

3. Pour into a well-greased Dutch oven and bake.

CORNMEAL MUFFIN LOAF

425°

Oven time: 25–30 minutes

1 cup flour
½ cup cornmeal
1 tablespoon baking powder
1 tablespoon sugar
½ teaspoon salt
1 tablespoon cooking oil
¾ cup milk
1 egg

1. Mix the flour, cornmeal, baking powder, sugar, and salt.

2. In a separate bowl, mix the cooking oil, milk, and egg. Add to the dry mix.

3. Bake in a greased Dutch oven until brown.

EASY CORNMEAL MUFFINS

450°

Oven time: Preheat 15 minutes
Bake 10–15 minutes

1 can refrigerator biscuits
½ cup cornmeal

1. Roll the biscuits in the cornmeal.

2. Place in a greased Dutch oven and bake until brown.

MEXICAN CORN BREAD

450°

Oven time: 40–50 minutes

3 eggs
2½ cups milk
3 cups cornmeal
4 slices bacon, cooked crisp and crumbled (save the grease)
¼ cup grated Cheddar cheese
1 7-ounce can whole corn
l large onion, chopped
¼ cup peanuts, chopped
½ cup chopped green pepper

1. Mix the eggs, milk, cornmeal, crumbled bacon, and half of the bacon grease.

2. Add the grated cheese, corn, onion, peanuts, and green pepper. Mix well.

3. Pour the remaining half of the bacon grease into a Dutch oven, add the mixture, and bake until golden brown.

SUGGESTED MENU
Pork sausage patties
Grapefruit
Mashed potatoes
Sauerkraut
Carrot sticks
Mexican Corn Bread
Blueberry cobbler

CORNMEAL BITS

Oven time: Boil in deep fat until bits float.

4 cups cooking oil
2 cups yellow cornmeal
2 tablespoons flour
1 teaspoon baking soda
1 teaspoon baking powder
1 teaspoon salt
½ cup extra-fine-chopped onion
1 egg
2 cups buttermilk

1. Pour the cooking oil into a Dutch oven and bring to a boil.

2. Combine the cornmeal, flour, soda, baking powder, and salt.

3. Add the onion, egg, and buttermilk.

4. Beat together and drop by rounded teaspoonfuls into hot cooking oil. The bits will float when they're done. Have the rest of the meal ready and eat them while they're warm.

PLAN AHEAD

Check your recipe before you start to cook. Have all utensils assembled, nuts chopped, sauces made, chocolate melted, seasonings mixed, shortening melted.

Cakes, Pies, and Desserts

CAKE MIXES

350°

Oven time: Preheat 15 minutes
Bake 20–30 minutes

A simple box of cake mix can be used to bake a really good cake in your Dutch oven. Here are some tips:

- Add water and eggs as directed on the package, beat two hundred to three hundred strokes, then pour the batter into an ungreased Dutch oven.

- You can bake a cake starting with the oven cold, but for best results the oven should be preheated at least 15 minutes.

- Most cakes will take 20 to 30 minutes to bake.

- A good way to test for doneness is to lightly press the cake's top with your finger. If the impression bounces back up, the cake is done.

Try not to open the oven more than once or twice during the cooking period. This will save heat and provide for more even baking.

APPLE PECAN CAKE

400°

Oven time: 45–60 minutes

2½ cups flour
3 cups pared, cored, and chopped apples
1 cup cooking oil
1 teaspoon vanilla
2 cups sugar
2 eggs
1 cup pecans

Blend all the ingredients together, pour into a Dutch oven, and bake.

APRICOT NECTAR CAKE

400°

Oven time: 45–60 minutes

1 12-ounce box yellow cake mix
1 12-ounce can apricot nectar
4 eggs
¼ cup lemon juice
¼ cup shortening, melted

1. Stir the cake mix, apricot nectar, eggs, and lemon juice together until smooth.

2. Stir in the shortening.

3. Pour into a Dutch oven and bake.

DARK MARSHMALLOW CAKE

350°

Oven time: 40–50 minutes

2 sticks (1 cup) margarine
4 eggs
2 cups sugar
⅛ teaspoon salt
1½ cups flour
1 teaspoon vanilla
½ cup cocoa
1½ cups pecan pieces
1 1-pound package small marshmallows

1. Melt the margarine.

2. Mix the eggs, sugar, salt, flour, vanilla, and cocoa.

3. Add the margarine to the cocoa mixture and blend.

4. Add the pecan pieces.

5. Bake in a greased Dutch oven.

6. Remove the lid when the cake is done and let it cool slightly.

7. Ice with the following icing, then place the marshmallows on top.

Icing

½ stick (¼ cup) margarine
⅓ cup cocoa
1 16-ounce box powdered sugar
1 teaspoon vanilla
¼ cup milk
⅛ teaspoon salt

1. Melt the margarine with the cocoa.

2. Stir in the powdered sugar, vanilla, milk, and salt, making a smooth mixture.

3. Spread on a cake.

BUTTERSCOTCH CAKE

350°

Oven time: 25–35 minutes

1 stick (½ cup) margarine, melted
1½ cups brown sugar
2 eggs, beaten well
⅛ teaspoon salt
1 teaspoon vanilla
1½ cups flour
2 teaspoons baking powder
1½ cups pecans, chopped

1. Blend the melted margarine and sugar.

2. Add the eggs, salt, and vanilla and mix thoroughly.

3. In a separate bowl, blend the flour, baking powder, and pecans. Stir lightly into the first mixture.

4. Pour into a greased Dutch oven and bake.

5. Cut into squares to serve.

SUGGESTED MENU
Broiled steak
Shrimp cocktail
Baked potatoes
Buttered beets
French bread
Tossed salad
Butterscotch Cake

EASY FRUIT CAKE

350°

Oven time: 1½–2 hours

1½ cups water
1 1-pound, 11-ounce jar mincemeat
2 eggs, beaten
1 12-ounce can sweetened condensed milk
2 cups mixed candied fruits
1 cup pecans, chopped
2½ cups flour
1 teaspoon baking soda

1. Pour the water into a Dutch oven.

2. Add the mincemeat to the water.

3. Bring to a boil and boil for 1 minute.

4. Remove from the heat and fold in the beaten eggs, condensed milk, fruit, and nuts.

5. In a separate bowl, stir the flour and soda together. Sprinkle and fold lightly into the fruit mixture and bake.

MEASURING FLOUR

Here's how to measure flour:

- **Regular flour.** Dip a measuring cup into the container and strike off the top. Do not tap the cup or pack the flour.
- **Cake flour.** Spoon cake flour into the cup to overflowing, then strike off.

LEMON-ORANGE CAKE

350°

Oven time: Preheat 15 minutes
Bake 40–50 minutes

1 box lemon cake mix
1 small package vanilla instant pudding
4 eggs
½ cup cooking oil
1 cup water

1. Blend the cake mix, pudding mix, eggs, cooking oil, and water. Beat at least 150 strokes.

2. Pour the mixture into a Dutch oven and bake until a toothpick comes out clean. Top with the following icing.

Icing

2 teaspoons margarine
½ cup orange juice
3 cups powdered sugar

1. Melt the margarine and mix with the orange juice and powdered sugar.

2. Punch holes in the top of the cake and pour the icing over the top.

3. Let set 10 or 15 minutes before serving.

STRAWBERRY CAKE

350°

Oven time: 30–45 minutes

1 16-ounce box frozen strawberries
2 12-ounce boxes white cake mix
¾ cup cooking oil
½ cup water
4 eggs
1 small package strawberry gelatin
1 stick (½ cup) margarine
1 16-ounce box powdered sugar

1. Thaw the strawberries, and divide them into two parts.

2. Blend the cake mixes, one part of the strawberries, the oil and the water well.

3. Blend in the eggs one at a time, beating after each addition.

4. Add the gelatin and beat well.

5. Pour into a greased and floured Dutch oven and bake.

6. Melt the margarine. Add the powdered sugar and remaining strawberries, and spread over the warm cake.

PINEAPPLE NUT CAKE

350°

Oven time: Preheat 15 minutes
Bake 50–60 minutes

1 8-ounce can crushed pineapple
2 cups flour
1 cup sugar
2 eggs, beaten
1½ teaspoons baking soda
¼ teaspoon cinnamon
¼ teaspoon mace
1 cup pecans, chopped
⅓ cup margarine, melted

1. Mix all the ingredients lightly until moistened through.

2. Pour into a greased, preheated Dutch oven and bake until the cake tests done and is brown.

3. Let sit 15 or 20 minutes before serving.

SUGGESTED MENU

Boneless beef roast
Orange sections
Fried noodles
Carrots
Bread
Pineapple Nut Cake

WALDORF ASTORIA RED CAKE

350°

Oven time: 35 minutes

½ cup shortening
1½ cups sugar
2 ounces red food coloring
2 eggs
1 tablespoon cocoa
2½ cups flour
1 teaspoon salt
1 teaspoon vanilla
1 cup buttermilk
1 teaspoon vinegar
1 teaspoon baking soda

1. Cream the shortening and sugar.

2. Add all the other ingredients and beat until smooth.

3. Pour into two layer pans and bake. Cool before serving, topping with the following frosting.

Frosting

1 cup milk
½ cup flour
1 cup sugar
1 cup shortening
Salt
Vanilla

1. Cook the milk with the flour, stirring constantly. When thick, set aside until very cool.

2. Cream the sugar and shortening. Add to the white sauce and beat until fluffy, adding salt and vanilla to taste.

Variation: Add coconut to give a different flavor.

"REAL" POUND CAKE

375°

Oven time: 1–1¼ hours

3 cups sugar
1½ sticks (¾ cup) margarine
¾ cup shortening
1 teaspoon rum flavoring or vanilla
9 eggs
2 cups flour

1. Cream the sugar, margarine, shortening, and flavoring with a fork.

2. Add the eggs one at a time, alternating them with the flour; end with flour. Beat until smooth.

3. Grease a Dutch oven well with shortening and sprinkle with flour.

4. Pour the batter into the oven and bake until brown.

SUGGESTED MENU

Spare ribs
Green beans with mushrooms
Cucumber-onion salad
Hard rolls
"Real" Pound Cake

TRAIL FUDGEES

350°

Oven time: 30–40 minutes

½ stick (¼ cup) margarine
1 cup sugar
1 teaspoon vanilla
2 eggs, beaten
2 1-ounce squares unsweetened chocolate, melted
½ cup flour
½ cup pecans, chopped

1. Cream the margarine, sugar, and vanilla.

2. Add the beaten eggs.

3. Blend in the chocolate.

4. Stir in the flour and nuts and bake.

5. Cool and cut into pieces.

CHOCOLATE SUBSTITUTE

Use 3 tablespoons cocoa plus 1 teaspoon margarine for each 1-ounce square of unsweetened chocolate called for in a recipe.

BLUEBERRY PUFF

350°

Oven time: 30 minutes

2 cups Jiffy baking mix
2 cups sugar
2 eggs, beaten
2 tablespoons cooking oil
2 cups milk
2 cups blueberries (frozen or fresh)

1. Thoroughly mix all the ingredients except the blueberries.

2. Fold in the blueberries and bake until brown.

FRESH WHOLE MILK SUBSTITUTES

To replace fresh whole milk, try any of the following:

- ½ cup evaporated milk plus ½ cup water.

- 1 cup reconstituted nonfat dry milk plus 2 tablespoons melted margarine or butter.

- 1 cup sour milk or buttermilk plus ½ teaspoon baking soda; decrease the baking powder in the recipe by 2 teaspoons.

TRAIL BUTTER COOKIES

350°

Oven time: 15–20 minutes

1 cup butter or margarine
2 cups flour
½ cup sugar
1 cup pecans or other nuts, chopped

1. Mix all the ingredients thoroughly.

2. Roll or pat out the dough to ½ inch thick.

3. Trim and shape to fit into the bottom of a Dutch oven. Bake.

4. Cut the cookies into serving-size pieces while hot.

5. Repeat until you run out of dough.

Variation: If desired, you can make these cookies into sandwiches with jam or jelly in the center, or sprinkle them with powdered sugar.

SUGGESTED MENU
Creamed dried beef on biscuits
Fried eggplant
Fruit salad
Trail Butter Cookies

BLUEBERRY BISCUIT CAKE

400°

Oven time: Preheat 15 minutes
Bake 20–30 minutes

2 cups baking mix
⅔ cup milk
4 tablespoons sugar
1 15-ounce can blueberries

1. Mix the baking mix and milk together thoroughly with a fork.

2. Pat out half the dough to fit the bottom of a Dutch oven.

3. Sprinkle 2 tablespoons of the sugar over the dough.

4. Drain the blueberries, saving the liquid.

5. Pour the blueberries into the oven and cover with the remaining half of dough—which has been patted into a sheet about ½ inch thick.

6. Sprinkle 2 tablespoons of sugar on top of the dough.

7. After tucking in the sides of the dough, pour the liquid from the blueberries on top.

8. Close the oven and bake.

GINGERBREAD

350°

Oven time: 35–45 minutes

¼ cup margarine
¼ cup shortening
½ cup sugar
1 egg
1 cup molasses
2½ cups flour
1½ teaspoons baking soda
1 teaspoon cinnamon
1 teaspoon ginger
½ teaspoon ground cloves
½ teaspoon salt
1 cup water

1. Cream the margarine, shortening, and sugar.

2. In a separate bowl, beat the egg and molasses together.

3. In a third bowl, mix the flour, baking soda, cinnamon, ginger, cloves, and salt.

4. Heat the water to boiling.

5. Mix all the ingredients together, then add the hot water, blending until smooth.

6. Pour into a greased Dutch oven and bake.

CHERRY FUDGE GOODIES

350°

Oven time: 30–40 minutes

1 box (approximately 18 ounces) brownie mix
1½ cups shredded coconut
1½ cups chopped candied cherries

1. Follow the brownie mix recipe.

2. Add the coconut and cherries and blend.

3. Pour the batter into a greased Dutch oven.

4. Bake until the brownies pull away from the sides of the oven (don't overcook).

5. Cut into squares to serve.

COCOA SQUARES

350°

Oven time: 20–30 minutes

1 stick (½ cup) margarine (or butter, if you'd like a richer cake)
1 cup flour
1 cup sugar
¼ cup cocoa
2 eggs

1. Cream the margarine or butter with a fork.

2. Stir the flour, sugar, and cocoa together.

3. Beat the eggs into the margarine and flour mix, blending thoroughly.

4. Spread the mixture in a Dutch oven and bake.

GRAHAM CRACKER BARS

250°–350°

Oven time: 15 minutes

½ pound graham crackers, crushed
1 cup chocolate chips
1½ cup coconut
1 cup sweetened condensed milk
1 teaspoon vanilla

1. Blend all the ingredients together.

2. Press into a greased Dutch oven.

3. Bake in a warm oven only. The ingredients burn easily if the oven is too hot.

4. Cut into bars to serve.

Note: Because all the ingredients are precooked, the cake need only be heated through.

SUGGESTED MENU

Pork sausage patties
Baked apples
Macaroni and cheese
Lettuce salad
Graham Cracker Bars

PIECRUST

2 cups flour
½ teaspoon salt
⅔ cup shortening
Water

1. Be sure the shortening and water are cool.

2. Cut the shortening into the flour and salt until the mixture is coarse and granular.

3. Add the cold water a little at a time, just enough to hold the mixture together, tossing with fork until all the granules are moistened.

4. Press into a ball and divide into two parts.

5. Roll out the dough on a cloth or lightly floured board, using short strokes toward the edges, to about ⅛ inch thick. Do not turn the dough over while you roll. If it sticks, lift it with a knife or spatula and dust the board with a small amount of flour.

6. Make a bottom crust 3 inches larger than the Dutch oven bottom, allowing it to come up the sides to tuck in for a pie.

7. Make a top crust 1 inch larger to allow for creasing around the edge.

8. Fold the dough in half, lift it carefully to place in the oven, then unfold.

APPLE CRUMB PIE

350°

Oven time: 30–45 minutes

3 cups peeled, cored, and diced apples
1 cup white sugar
2 cups brown sugar
1 cup flour
1 stick (½ cup) margarine, melted

1. Place the apples in a Dutch oven and pour white sugar over the top.

2. Let stand 15 minutes.

3. Mix together the brown sugar, flour, and melted margarine.

4. Pour over the apples and bake until golden brown.

SUGGESTED MENU

Short spare ribs
Asparagus
Hash brown potatoes
Hard rolls
Wilted lettuce
Apple Crumb Pie

APPLE SHARPY

350°

Oven time: 30 minutes

2 cups pie-sliced apples
1 teaspoon cinnamon
1 teaspoon nutmeg
2 tablespoons lemon juice
¾ cup margarine
2½ cups brown sugar
1 cup flour

1. Drain the apple slices, saving the juice, and pour into a greased Dutch oven.

2. Sprinkle the apples with cinnamon, nutmeg, and lemon juice.

3. Pour ½ cup of apple juice over the mixture.

4. Soften margarine and blend it with the brown sugar and flour, mixing until crumbly.

5. Sprinkle over the apples and bake. This dessert can be served with milk, cream (whipped or plain), or ice cream.

EASY APPLE BAKE
350°
Oven time: 30 minutes

2 15- or 16-ounce cans apple pie slices
1 stick (½ cup) margarine, sliced into small pieces
2½ cups graham cracker crumbs

1. Mix all the ingredients in a Dutch oven and bake.

2. Serve with whipped topping.

APPLE PIE
450°
Oven time: 40–50 minutes

Piecrust
6 cups pared, sliced apples (¼ inch slices)
⅔ cup sugar
¼ teaspoon nutmeg
⅛ teaspoon salt
¼ teaspoon cinnamon
1 teaspoon lemon juice
2 teaspoons margarine

1. Place a piecrust bottom in a Dutch oven.

2. Fill the crust with apple slices.

3. Mix the sugar, nutmeg, salt, cinnamon, and lemon juice.
Pour over the apple slices.

4. Lay the top crust on.

5. Crimp the edges with your fingers or a floured fork.

6. Cut holes in the top crust to let out steam.

7. Brush the top with melted margarine.

8. Bake until golden brown.

BLUEBERRY PIE

400°

Oven time: 40–50 minutes

Follow the Apple Pie recipe but substitute for the apples 4 cups blue-berries, along with 2 tablespoons of flour or 2 tablespoons of quick-cooking tapioca.

Note: Blackberries, raspberries, plums, grapes, rhubarb or peaches may be used in the same way. Some tart fruits may require a bit more sugar.

PEACH CREAM PIE

400°

Oven time: 35–50 minutes

Piecrust
3 cups peeled and sliced peaches (or canned peaches
in light syrup, drained)
¼ cup flour
¾ cup sugar
¼ teaspoon salt
¼ teaspoon nutmeg
1 cup half-and-half

1. Prepare a single piecrust 3 inches larger than your Dutch oven.

2. Place in the oven and crimp the edge.

3. Place the peaches in the crust.

4. Combine the flour, sugar, salt, and nutmeg and sprinkle over the peaches.

5. Pour half-and-half over the mixture and bake until firm.

6. Chill before serving.

PUMPKIN PIE

375°

Oven time: 50–60 minutes

Piecrust
1 1-pound can pumpkin
1 14-ounce can sweetened condensed milk
¼ teaspoon cinnamon
½ teaspoon ginger
½ teaspoon nutmeg
½ teaspoon salt
1 egg

1. Prepare a single piecrust and place in a Dutch oven.

2. Crimp the edge with your fingers or a fork.

3. Mix all the ingredients together, pour into the crust, and bake.

WASHINGTON'S FAVORITE

350°

Oven time: 30 minutes

2 cups apple pie filling
1 bowl Jiffy white cake mix
1 stick (½ cup) margarine

1. Pour the apple pie filling into a greased Dutch oven.

2. Spread the dry cake mix over the top evenly.

3. Dot with margarine and bake. Serve warm.

FRESH BLACKBERRY COBBLER
350°
Oven time: 30 minutes

2 quarts fresh blackberries
½ cup lemon juice
¼ teaspoon salt
2 cups sugar
1 box Jiffy yellow cake mix
1 stick (½ cup) margarine
1 cup chopped nuts

1. Spread the berries in a greased Dutch oven.

2. Mix the lemon juice, salt, and sugar. Pour over the berries.

3. Sprinkle the cake mix evenly over the top and dot with the margarine.

4. Top with nuts and bake.

MEASURING BROWN SUGAR
Pack brown sugar into a dry measuring cup until firm enough to hold its shape when you turn it out of the cup.

TRAIL DATE-NUT PUDDING

350°

Oven time: Preheat 15 minutes
Bake 30–40 minutes

3 eggs
1 cup sugar
¼ cup flour
1 teaspoon baking powder
¼ teaspoon salt
2½ cups dates, chopped
1 cup pecans, chopped (other nuts may be used)

1. Beat the eggs until light and fluffy.

2. Slowly add the sugar and beat until the batter becomes very thick.

3. Mix in the flour, baking powder, and salt.

4. Mix in the dates and nuts.

5. Pour into a greased Dutch oven and bake.

6. Serve warm, plain or with topping.

SUGGESTED MENU
Sauerkraut and hot dogs
French fries
Green beans
Bread rolls
Tomatoes
Trail Date-Nut Pudding

WOODY'S FAMOUS MEMPHIS MOLLY

350°

Oven time: 20–30 minutes

1 15-ounce can tart cherries
1 15-ounce can unsweetened crushed pineapple
1 box Jiffy white cake mix
½ stick (¼ cup) margarine
All the pecans you can afford

1. Pour the cherries and pineapple into a Dutch oven and stir.
2. Sprinkle the cake mix over the fruit.
3. Spread flakes of margarine over the top.
4. Spread pecans over the top and bake.

SORGHUM MOLASSES NO-CRUST PIE

350°

Oven time: Preheat 15 minutes
Bake 30–40 minutes

3 eggs
1 teaspoon lemon juice
½ teaspoon salt
1 cup sugar
2 tablespoons flour
1 cup sorghum molasses
¼ cup margarine, melted
½ cup pecans

1. Beat the eggs in a Dutch oven.
2. Add the lemon juice, salt, sugar, flour, and sorghum, beating.
3. Stir in the pecans and melted margarine and bake.

PINE-RICE DESSERT

350°

Oven time: 20–25 minutes

1 cup extra-long-grain rice
2 cups water
1 teaspoon salt
1 15-ounce can crushed pineapple, drained (save juice)
1 teaspoon cooking oil
½ stick (¼ cup) margarine
½ cup brown sugar

1. Combine in a Dutch oven the rice, water, salt, pineapple juice, and cooking oil.

2. Bring to a boil.

3. Slow the oven temperature and simmer 15 minutes.

4. Melt the margarine and add the brown sugar.

5. Add the pineapple to the margarine mixture and glaze 3 minutes.

6. Add layers of rice and glazed pineapple with juices into the Dutch oven and simmer 5 minutes. Serve warm.

SUGGESTED MENU

Swiss steak
Orange juice
Boiled whole small potatoes
Carrots
Corn bread
Pine-Rice Dessert

APPLE SPICE DESSERT

350°

Oven time: 20 minutes

2 15-ounce cans applesauce
1 box Jiffy spice cake mix
½ cup chopped pecans
1 stick (½ cup) margarine

1. Pour the applesauce into a greased Dutch oven.

2. Spread the dry cake mix evenly over the top.

3. Sprinkle pecans on top of the mix.

4. Dot margarine over the top and bake.

BAKED APPLES

350°

Oven time: 30 minutes

8 apples, cored
1 16-ounce sugar-free strawberry, orange, or
cherry soda pop

1. Place the apples in a Dutch oven.

2. Pour the soda over the apples and bake.

Variation: Cinnamon or nutmeg may be sprinkled over the apples before baking.

Condiments

HERB SEASONING
(Salt Substitute)

1 tablespoon garlic powder
½ teaspoon cayenne pepper
1 teaspoon basil
1 teaspoon marjoram
1 teaspoon thyme
1 teaspoon parsley
1 teaspoon savory
1 teaspoon mace
1 teaspoon onion powder
1 teaspoon black pepper
1 teaspoon sage
1 teaspoon cumin
1 teaspoon cinnamon
1 teaspoon lemon peel

Place in a salt shaker and use as much as you desire on vegetables, meats, and poultry.

MORE SALT SUBSTITUTES
Vinegar, lime juice, and lemon juice also make good substitutes for salt.

 **CUCUMBER SAUCE**

Grate a cucumber and season with cider vinegar to taste.

 **CURRY SAUCE**

1 tablespoon cooking oil or margarine
1 teaspoon onion juice
1 tablespoon curry powder
2 tablespoons flour
2 cups skim milk
⅛ teaspoon herb seasoning

1. Mix together the first four ingredients, stirring until smooth.

2. Heat the milk to a boil and stir into the mixture, adding the herb seasoning.

 SWEET PEPPER SAUCE

2 tablespoons cooking oil or margarine
¼ teaspoon garlic powder
½ teaspoon diced onion
1 tablespoon flour
1 cup boiling water
1 cup chopped sweet pepper
¼ teaspoon salt
⅛ teaspoon pepper
½ teaspoon minced parsley

1. Stir together the oil, garlic, and onion, cooking until brown.

2. Stir in the flour, water, and sweet pepper.

3. Stir in the salt, pepper, and parsley.

4. Bring to a boil and serve hot.

 # BROWN SAUCE

2 tablespoons cooking oil or margarine
½ medium onion, diced fine
2 tablespoons flour
2 cups hot water
1 salt-free beef bouillon cube

1. Mix the oil and onion together and brown.

2. Blend in the flour.

3. Dissolve the bouillon cube in the hot water. Add to the mixture and stir until smooth.

LEMON BUTTER

4 tablespoons margarine, melted
1 teaspoon lemon juice
⅛ teaspoon pepper

Blend all the ingredients together and serve hot.

 # ONION SAUCE

1 tablespoon cooking oil or margarine
2 tablespoons sugar
2 onions, grated fine
⅛ teaspoon herb seasoning
1 tablespoon flour
2 cups water
1 tablespoon cider vinegar
1 salt-free beef bouillon cube

1. Brown the sugar in the oil. Add the onions and brown.

2. Add the flour and herb seasoning and brown.

3. Dissolve the bouillon cube and vinegar in the hot water, then add to the sauce.

4. Cook until smooth and creamy brown.

APPLE-HORSERADISH SAUCE

2 tablespoons white vinegar
3 apples, peeled
3 tablespoons horseradish
2 teaspoons sugar

1. Grate the peeled apples into the vinegar and blend.

2. Stir the horseradish and sugar into the mixture.

 **SAFFLOWER SALAD DRESSING**

¼ cup egg substitute
1 teaspoon cider vinegar
2 teaspoons fresh lemon juice
1 teaspoon mustard
¼ teaspoon salt
¼ cup olive oil
1 cup safflower oil

1. Combine all the ingredients except ½ cup of the safflower oil in a blender. Blend 2 minutes.

2. Add the second half of the oil and blend 2 minutes more.

VINEGAR AND OIL ZESTY DRESSING

½ cup cider vinegar
2 teaspoons lemon juice
½ cup safflower oil
⅛ teaspoon garlic powder
⅛ teaspoon onion powder
Dash hot sauce
2 teaspoons brown sugar

Blend all the ingredients and use as soon as possible.

Variation: You can vary this recipe in as many ways as you desire. Have fun and use your imagination!

WOODY'S BBQ SAUCE

(Makes enough to share with your neighbors)

This fine BBQ sauce—which takes just a few minutes and little effort to prepare—can be made and stored for a long time in your cupboard. The quantities are not firm; go ahead and change them if you wish a more pronounced taste of a particular spice. Try this recipe first, then branch out on your own.

Oven time: Simmer 30 minutes

½ teaspoon black pepper

1 cup brown sugar

1 teaspoon chili powder

½ teaspoon cinnamon

½ teaspoon cumin

¼ teaspoon garlic powder

½ cup honey

½ teaspoon hot sauce

½ teaspoon onion powder

¼ teaspoon oregano

1 teaspoon salt

½ cup sorghum molasses

½ cup sour orange juice or lime juice

¼ teaspoon tarragon

½ cup vinegar

1 cup water

Mix all the ingredients in a Dutch oven bottom and bring to a slow boil. Let simmer for 30 minutes; either use at once or store until needed.

GRANDDAD WOODY'S OLD-FASHIONED APPLE BUTTER

350°

Oven time: 1¼–1¾ hours

6 pounds apples, diced (leave peels and seeds in)
½ gallon sweet untreated cider
1 teaspoon cinnamon
½ teaspoon nutmeg
½ teaspoon allspice
½ cup candy red hots
3 cups sugar

1. Fill a Dutch oven with cider to ½ inch from the top and boil down until reduced by half. Add the apples and cook until they mash up, stirring occasionally.

2. Run the pulp and juice through a strainer and return to the Dutch oven to bake.

3. Stir the mix occasionally to keep it from burning, especially as it thickens.

4. When the pulp has been baking 45 minutes, add all the spices, candies, and sugar. Stir thoroughly.

5. Test by dropping a drop on a cold plate. Apple butter is ready when it is thick, and not watery around the edge.

STORING APPLE BUTTER

Apple butter will keep for a reasonable amount of time in the refrigerator. You can also freeze it—but chances are it'll be all used up before you have time to do so, especially if you spread it on good Dutch oven biscuits.

Index

M

Macaroni
  and cheese, 104
  cheesit with beef, 19
Marshmallow cake, dark, 138
Meal in an oven, 34
Meat and potato casserole, 23
Meat loaf, 12, 13
Mexican corn bread, 132
Mini meal sirloin balls, 15
Molasses
  bread, 118
  no-crust pie with sorghum, 159
Muffins
  cornmeal, 131
  cornmeal loaf, 131
  roll loaf, 117

Mushroom(s)
  mini sandwiches, 105
  pork steak, 30
  with green beans, 71
  with peas, 86
  with turkey, 47

N

Noodles
  romanoff, 106
  with beef, 20
  with cheese, 102
  with tuna, 57
  with veal stew, 25
Nut(s)
  pudding, with dates, 160
  with banana bread, 114